YOUR .... WAYNE NATIONAL FOREST

VOL. I

A Collection of the Author's Newspaper Columns from 1981 and 1982

By Dan Kincaid

ISBN 13:978-1523612956

ISBN 10:1523612959

Published by: Kade Holley Publishing and Create Space

Editing: Shannon Lough and Kade Holley

Cover design: Kenn Kincaid.com and Kade Holley Publishing

Cover photo courtesy of USDA Forest Service

Printed in the United States of America.

REVIEWS AND READER COMMENTS:

Dan Kincaid's weekly columns were very helpful in communicating between the Wayne National Forest and local residents. His efforts during the 1980s helped foster a positive working relationship that was sorely needed at the time. I consider Dan to be a good friend and these stories bring back fond memories of those days, when we eagerly looked forward to another interesting topic each week.

Jack Haessly, President, Haessly Hardwood Lumber Company, Marietta, Ohio

Dan and his staff worked closely with our students on forestry education. They took a sincere interest in Frontier High School and the entire district to help everyone understand the value of and the role of the Wayne National Forest. Dan really meant it when he told us that he wanted the Wayne to be a good neighbor. This book brings back great memories of those times.

Calvin Martin, retired FFA Advisor and Vocational Instructor, Frontier High School

Dan's book is an important addition to the historical record of our area. Natural resources and the Wayne National Forest are key components of southeastern Ohio's landscape. These columns feature topics that were important in the early 1980s. Future generations will be glad that these columns have been captured in this book.

Bill Reynolds, Historian, Friends of the Museum-Ohio History Connection, Marietta

DEDICATION

This book is dedicated to Lacy Johnson and Al Wolter, two former employees of the U.S. Forest Service and the Wayne National Forest. Both were dedicated foresters, educated and trained in the science of forestry, who made significant contributions to the management of forest resources in southeastern Ohio. In addition, each one understood the value and importance of communicating with the public about the activities of the Wayne National Forest.

Johnson wrote newspaper columns in the Marietta area and Wolter in the Ironton area. Their columns, written in the 1970's, helped readers to better understand natural resource and national forest management. Each of these men was a friend and a mentor to me as I began a 10-year journey as a weekly outdoor newspaper columnist in Ohio.

- Dan Kincaid

PREFACE AND ACKNOWLEDGEMENTS

The leadership of The Marietta Times newspaper was extremely helpful and encouraging to me during the decade that I wrote the column, ***Your....Wayne National Forest***. In particular, Managing Editor George Freeman was a tremendous supporter of my efforts.

Two weekly newspapers in Monroe County - The Spirit of Democracy and The Monroe County Beacon - also ran my columns. Pam Sloan, Publisher of The Beacon, was especially helpful and supporting over the years.

My columns appeared less regularly in the Logan Daily News and the Athens Messenger, as well as occasionally in other Ohio and West Virginia newspapers in the mid-Ohio Valley.

My supervisors at the Wayne National Forest, especially in the early years, offered support and encouragement for my efforts. In particular, Bob Joens, District Ranger at Athens, who was my immediate supervisor, and Harold Godlevske, Forest Supervisor, were instrumental in their support of the columns. They recognized the value to the U.S. Forest Service of communicating with the public via regular newspaper columns.

Readers, especially in Washington and Monroe counties, responded favorably to my columns, offering thanks and encouragement, and often suggesting topics for future columns. Reader feedback was important in newspaper decisions to continue carrying the columns.

From January 1981 until mid-1990, I wrote a total of 469 columns. There were always a couple of weeks each year when I did not write a column for various reasons – holidays, vacations, etc. During 1990, as I was preparing to leave Ohio for another job in Kentucky, I only wrote 22 columns.

This book includes about 42 columns each from 1981 and 1982. I left out a few that did not seem of much value or contained similar information to other columns. Also, during the 10 years that I wrote these columns, I occasionally asked other people to write one; or I asked permission to include a column that someone else had written. A few of those are included in this volume.

On a couple of the February 1981 columns that follow, I have included a graphic to show how the headers appeared at the beginning of each column.

INTRODUCTION

Early in my career with the U.S. Forest Service, I began to realize how important the national forests were to the people living near them. Yes, citizens across the country valued the national forests, but, in particular, the management activities on the national forests affected the local residents the most. That is still the case today.

An effective means of communicating with large numbers of people, especially during the early years of my career in the 1970s and 1980s, was through regular newspaper columns. That allowed an opportunity for contact on a weekly basis and it allowed the opportunity to address numerous topics over the course of a year.

Other means of communications, such as news releases, one-on-one discussions, and community meetings were also important, but none offered the sustained contact with large numbers of people that weekly newspaper columns did.

I wrote weekly columns for about 12 years – two in Georgia and ten in Ohio. The feedback I received from readers and community leaders convinced me that the effort was worthwhile and valuable.

Although there have been similar efforts by other Forest Service employees across the country over the years, the numbers have been small. I only wish that these kinds of communications activities had received a higher priority by management. If they had, then perhaps some of the problems that the agency encountered with local communities might have been avoided.

As you will notice from reading the columns in this book, my topics ranged widely. I decided early on to include not only the specific Forest Service topics, but also topics on various natural resource and outdoor activities, as well as columns mentioning individuals, groups, and other agencies that would be of interest to readers. I figured that the greater the variety of topics, the greater the number of readers. And I wanted to give credit to those individuals who were doing noteworthy things in regard to the outdoors.

So, there were columns of national interest, but also of local interest. There were columns on: general topics; specific, detailed topics; professional forestry; explanations of Forest Service policies; explanations of differences between various state and federal agencies; and definitely some human interest stories. And as I mentioned earlier, this wide-ranging strategy must have worked because the reader response was overwhelmingly positive.

The columns in this book are what were submitted to the various newspapers. They may have differed slightly from the final versions that appeared in print. Also, the dates listed on each column were the submission dates, not the actual dates they appeared in the newspapers.

I hope you enjoy reading through these columns as much as I enjoyed writing them. It will give you a historical sense of what was going on some 35 years ago – in the Wayne National Forest, the great outdoors, and with natural resource issues of the time.

Oh, yes, one last comment. You may catch me ending some sentences with a preposition. That's okay; they often sound better that way. You'll see that I even mention it in one of my columns. And I like to capitalize the four seasons. There are too many other uses for the words spring and fall. To me, the seasons should be Spring and Fall, no matter what the dictionary says. If you would, please give me some slack on those things. I'd certainly appreciate it.

January 19, 1981 -

Beginning today, I'll be writing a weekly column that's intended to acquaint readers with their National Forests. Many of the articles will be centered around activities on southeastern Ohio's Wayne National Forest. We hope that you'll find this column both interesting and pertinent to your daily activities.

The Wayne National Forest is administered out of three area offices - Ironton, Athens, and Marietta. It is one of the country's newer National Forests, having been officially established in 1951. It is also perhaps the smallest of all the 155 National Forests. Indeed, it's a unique Forest offering many opportunities. Keep an eye on the column for information that may be of interest to you.

The Marietta Unit of the Wayne National Forest comprises over 43,000 acres - 28,000+ in Washington County and 14,000+ in Monroe County. As a concerned neighbor we realize that our policies and activities have some degree of impact on almost every resident of these two counties. We hope to provide information about our activities so you'll know what we're doing, how we're doing it, and most importantly, why we're doing it. We'll be providing information on programs we manage, assistance we offer, special activities, career opportunities, and a lot of just plain outdoor, forestry related items.

Other periodic features will include photographs and histories of our employees, some of whom you've known for years and others who are relative newcomers. Also many of the columns will end with an item of special interest titled "Ranger's Notebook," which will point out little known facts about the Forest Service and the profession of Forestry.

Well, that's enough for now. I hope you're looking forward to reading the column as much as I'm looking forward to writing it. Till next week, so long.

RANGER'S NOTEBOOK - The U.S. Forest Service manages 155 National Forests, 19 National Grasslands, and 17 Land Utilization Projects located in 44 states, Puerto Rico, and the Virgin Islands. These areas total over 187 million acres. The Wayne National Forest covers parts of 11 different counties, totaling 175,105 acres.

February 2, 1981 –

With the increased awareness and interest in the outdoors over the past few years, many people have found the need to call someone for information or answers to their questions. Trouble is, though, it's often difficult to figure out where to call. And that's perfectly understandable, with the many resource-related agencies that we have at the federal, state, county, and city levels. Though most of these agencies cooperate in certain land management activities, each one is an entirely separate organization with different responsibilities.

The Wayne National Forest is one of 155 National Forests in the United States, all of which are managed by the U.S. Forest Service. The Forest Service is part of the U.S. Department of Agriculture. Each National Forest is divided into Districts which are generally administered by Foresters, who are called "District Rangers, or Rangers." The Marietta Unit is part of the Athens District, administered by District Ranger Bob Joens.

The Wayne National Forest is a part of Region 9 - the Eastern Region of the U.S. Forest Service. This includes Forests in West Virginia, Pennsylvania, Maine, New Hampshire, Vermont, Michigan, Wisconsin, Minnesota, Missouri, Illinois, Ohio and Indiana.

We're often called the Wayne National Park, which is, of course, incorrect. There are no National Parks in this immediate area. National Parks are a part of the Department of Interior, a completely separate organization from ours. "Park rangers" administer activities at the National Parks.

National Forests are "working forests" which, by law, are managed for continuous yields of water, recreation, forage, timber, and wildlife. Other uses and activities on National Forests include fire management, land use planning, minerals/mining, environmental education, wilderness, transportation (roads & trails), and manpower work programs. National Parks, on the other hand, are managed basically under a system of preservation, primarily for recreational use. Examples of these are the Shenandoah National Park in the Blue Ridge Mountains of Virginia and the Grand Canyon National Park in Arizona.

Sometimes there's confusion between our duties and those of the State of Ohio employees. We often work together on certain items, but we have totally separate responsibilities. Game wardens, oil and gas inspectors, wildlife managers, and employees of State Parks and Forests all work for the State of Ohio. The Ohio Department of Natural Resources also has Foresters working in most counties. They give assistance to private landowners concerning forestry management. Our Wayne National Forest activities, with few exceptions, occur only on National Forest land. (In this area, that includes parts of eastern Washington County and southern Monroe County).

If you have questions concerning the Wayne National Forest or other outdoor activities, please stop by our office in Reno or call 373-9055. We'd be glad to help you; and if we can't, we'll surely help you get in touch with the proper agency. We want to help you better enjoy your..........Wayne National Forest.

RANGER'S NOTEBOOK - The National Forests were first authorized by the Creative Act of 1891. President Benjamin Harrison established an area of 1.2 million acres in Wyoming. The U.S. Forest Service first began acquiring land in southeastern Ohio in 1935. The Wayne National Forest was formally established on October 1, 1951.

February 9, 1981

Your Wayne National Forest

by Dan Kincaid

What's the state tree of Ohio? I'm sure most of you know, because Ohio has perhaps the most well-known state tree in the country - the Ohio buckeye. Our nickname is the "Buckeye State", and Ohio State University's sports teams are called the Buckeyes. So it's hard to go thru life as an Ohioan and not hear about the Buckeye tree.

Our neighboring states, however, don't enjoy the same exposure and publicity about their state trees. I mean, can you imagine West Virginia University's football team being called the "fighting Sugar Maples;" or how about the Michigan State White Pines. Sounds funny to me. And the Hoosier state, Indiana, just wouldn't seem right being called the "Yellow Poplar State".

What made me think about state trees was last week when I talked to two grade school kids. They were gathering information for a school report. One stopped by the office with questions about the Ohio buckeye and the other one called us to find out about state trees of our neighboring states. We searched around the office and came up with some interesting facts for them.

The Ohio buckeye is sometimes called "Fetid Buckeye" or "Smelly Buckeye" because of the unpleasant smell given off when the leaves and twigs are crushed. The leaves are easy to identify because of the 5 or 6 leaflets that occur on each leaf stem. It almost looks like the fingers and palm of someone's outstretched hand. Of course the best known feature of the tree is the buckeye "nut". This nut is actually the seed of the tree and grows in a shiny fruit pod which is covered with short, prickly points. (The fruit pod of its cousin, the yellow buckeye, is smooth with no sharp points). The fruit usually matures in October, when the seeds fall to the ground. Don't eat them however, because they're somewhat poisonous. The wood of the Ohio buckeye is light, soft, weak, and pale yellow. It is not an important timber tree, although it is sometimes used for pulpwood, woodenware, and occasionally for lumber.

West Virginia's state tree, the sugar maple, occurs throughout the eastern U.S., including Ohio. The sugar maple is widely planted as a shade tree and is well known for the maple sugar and syrup which is made by boiling down the sap. The wood is hard and is used for furniture, handles, crates, and flooring (including many bowling alleys and dance floors).

The state tree of Pennsylvania is the Eastern hemlock, an evergeen tree found in cool, moist areas. It's sometimes called "spruce pine". Young hemlocks are often planted for hedges. The wood is light, soft and not especially durable. It's mainly used for rough or construction lumber. Lew Morgenstern and I noticed some hemlocks growing along the Little Muskingum River a couple of months ago.

The Eastern white pine, Michigan's state tree, can grow to majestic heights, even over 100 feet. In early Colonial days the taller, straighter trees were marked as property of the King of England and were used as ship masts for their Navy. The wood is soft, light, and easily worked. It has a variety of uses including construction purposes, clocks, boxboards, and matches.

Indiana and Kentucky share the same state tree - the Yellow Poplar or Tulip Tree. The flower of the tree has yellowish-green petals with orange bands near the base and looks very much like a tulip. The tree grows very fast and often exceeds 100 feet in height. The wood is light and soft. It's commonly used for siding, trim, crates, musical instruments, picture frames, plywood, and veneer. The Tulip Tree is found throughout Ohio.

RANGER'S NOTEBOOK

Wood is such a major part of our lives that we sometimes take it for granted. On the average, each person uses more than 550 pounds of paper and 200 board feet of timber every year. We're lucky that, unlike fossil fuels, wood is a renewable resource - trees can be harvested, utilized and then replanted for the future.

February 16, 1981

by Dan Kincaid

Winter hunting, camping, and hiking are enjoyable activities for many people; but they can also be very dangerous, or even fatal, if necessary preparations are not made or proper precautions are not taken. In the summertime minor errors in judgment usually result in only slight inconveniences. However, in the wintertime these same mistakes accumulate and multiply rapidly, with sometimes tragic results. The following thoughts should be useful to the winter outdoorsman:

1. Travel with a group, or at least with a partner. Then, in case of sickness or injury someone can go for help.

2. Lay out a reasonable travel route. Generally speaking, most people think they can walk much further than they actually can. With winter days

being very short and snow accumulation slowing your rate of speed, don't over estimate the distance that you plan to travel. If you're camping, be sure to set up camp early and not get caught by darkness.

3. Know your route well. Be aware of possible hazards. In this part of the country it is best to stay off of lakes or ponds even if the ice appears to be thick enough to walk on. A plunge in icy water, away from help, can be fatal.

4. Be prepared for the worst: Besides the cold temperatures, the winds are often very strong, particularly on mountains or ridge tops. Extreme wind chill factors can worsen the consequences of any problems you might encounter. At 10 degrees (F) above zero a 25 mile per hour wind causes the chill factor to be 30 degrees below zero! In this instance exposed flesh can freeze within a very few minutes.

5. Be sure to let someone know where you're going and when you plan to return. If you're not back on time, rescuers will have an idea where to make their search.

6. Make sure your vehicle is in good winter driving condition. When you get ready to come home, a car that won't start can spoil your whole trip.

7. Drink plenty of liquids. Dehydration is more common in extreme cold. An adult, at rest, requires about 2 quarts of water daily. Up to 4 quarts are required for strenuous activity. There is a 25% loss of stamina when an adult loses $1^1/_2$ quarts of water. Avoid dehydration - simply drink as often as you feel thirsty.

8. If you're cold, eat something, drink something warm, and put on a cap. Most of the body's heat loss occurs thru the head.

9. Stay dry! When cloths get wet, they lose up to 90% of their insulating value. Wool is the exception. It retains a lot of its insulating value even when wet. So, if you're going to be out when it's both wet and cold, wool is your best bet. A waterproof windbreaker is very useful in helping to stay warm and dry.

Winter days can be very beautiful. To make sure you have an enjoyable outing:

1) Be prepared; 2) Take necessary precautions; and, 3) Respect nature's rules.

RANGER'S NOTEBOOK - Hypothermia is the number one killer of outdoor recreationists. It is a subnormal body temperature which, if not reversed, leads to mental and physical collapse. It is caused by exposure to cold, wet, and wind, thus causing body heat loss. A word of warning -- most cases of hypothermia occur in air temperatures between 30 and 50 degrees (F) above zero and during rainy weather; so, you can have problems not only in the winter, but also in the Spring and Fall.

February 23, 1981 -

We get a lot of questions here at the office concerning the profession of Forestry and other related fields. Many people wonder what a Forester, or Forest Ranger, actually does. Here are three of the most frequently asked questions:

"What does a Forester do?"

Many people think Foresters either sit in fire towers all day long watching for fires, or spend all day cutting trees down like the old lumberjacks. While Foresters do indeed spot fires and help harvest timber, these are but two of the many activities in which they get involved. A Forester is trained to perform a wide variety of jobs which relate to the management and protection of natural resources. This includes wildlife management, insect and disease control, recreation management, fire fighting, land line surveying, timber inventory, water and soil protection, landscape architecture, environmental education, and many other areas as well.

The Forester uses his/her skills, and also consults with specialists, in order to make wise decisions for the proper use of forest land. In practice, the Forester is a "land manager."

"What type of training or experience is required for a forestry job?"

A love of the outdoors is the basic requirement for working in forestry. But don't think that it'll be all hunting, camping, fishing, and hiking. In fact, you'll find that you don't have as much time for these activities as you'd like, because you're too busy working to make sure others can enjoy them.

Educational requirements for Foresters vary slightly, but primarily there is strong emphasis on science and mathematics during your four years in college. Nearby schools that offer degrees in forestry are Ohio State, Purdue, Kentucky, West Virginia, Virginia Tech, and Penn State. Forestry Technicians work with Foresters in almost all management activities. Requirements for these positions are either graduating from a two-year Technical School or having a very strong background in outdoor, forestry-related work. Hocking Technical College in Nelsonville, Ohio and Glenville State College in Glenville, West Virginia both offer the two-year degrees. Washington County Vocational School offers a

Forestry curriculum for junior and senior high school students, also. One of their graduates, Duane Lowe, is currently working for us.

"Are there many job opportunities in the field of Forestry?"

Job opportunities are steadily increasing, but so is the competition for them. However, don't let that stop you. If your desire is strong enough, you'll land a job. In addition to the Federal government, there are opportunities in State, County, and City governments, private industry, and individual consulting work. It's difficult to cover everything in a short column; so if you have other questions, please stop by our office on Rt. 7 in Reno or call 373-9055.

RANGER'S NOTEBOOK - Bernhard E. Fernow was the first professional Forester in the United States. He received his education in Germany and taught the first forestry class in this country at Massachusetts Agricultural College in 1894. The Fernow Experimental Forest, a research area in West Virginia, was named after him.

March 2, 1981 -

Spring is in the air! Though I'm sure Ol' Man Winter won't go away without a couple of more chilly blasts, we've at least had enough of a glimpse at Springtime to ease our "cabin fever" somewhat. It won't be long until we'll see the redbud and dogwood trees blooming. And I've already heard several birds singing on these warmer mornings. Yessirree! Spring is just around the corner.

There's much beauty to behold during the Winter, but the coming of Spring seems to bring a certain joy to everyone's heart. The changing seasons -how lucky we are to be able to enjoy each one in its own special way.

Besides bringing warmer temperatures, longer days, animal activity, and baseball season, Spring also brings something that is dear to my heart -the tasty, delectable, wild ramp. This small plant, with the green top and the onion-like stem, is one of the pure delights of Springtime.

The ramp is found growing throughout the Appalachian Mountains, primarily in moist, shaded coves and in rich soil. Its green leaves are among the first to emerge from the forest floor after the long Winter. Young, tender ramps are the best ones to eat and these can be found from mid-April to early June, depending on what state you happen to live in. Much later than this and the ramps become too tough to eat.

Being a native of the West Virginia mountains, I was introduced to ramps at an early age. Other than cornbread and buttermilk, there's nothing my Dad would rather eat than ramps. Like father -- like son. A side benefit to eating ramps is that they are very high in vitamin C. This was very important to early mountain people because of the lack of other vitamin C foods in their Springtime diets.

Don't let anyone talk you into not eating ramps because of their supposedly strong taste or because their smell lingers on your breath somewhat longer than normal onions. In short, if you like onions of any kind (or prepared in any manner), then you'll like ramps. The ramp is a cook's delight since it is such a versatile food.

If you like raw onions, then you'll love ramps. Eat them with bread and butter, sprinkle them with salt, or try them my favorite way -- with cornbread and beans. Do you like french-fried onion rings? Great! Just cut off the leaves of your ramps, dip the stems in batter, throw them in the deep fryer and --- Presto! French-fried ramps. (This also takes a little of the nippiness out of their taste for those who don't like them raw). My wife won't eat them raw, but french-fried and dipped in ketchup ---- Um-umh. Other ways to prepare them? Take the tops that you just cut off and cook them like greens. If you want, add vinegar. How tasty! How about with scrambled eggs? Cut the ramps (tops and bottoms) into small pieces and scramble them in your eggs. What a delicious breakfast! Chop them up and add them to your tossed salad or fry them whole in bacon grease. These are only a few of the more popular ways to prepare ramps. If you have a favorite way to fix them that I haven't included here, please let me know. I'd love to try it.

RANGER'S NOTEBOOK - Ramps are found in many counties throughout Ohio. I've personally seen them in Lawrence and Gallia Counties, and my Dad knows where some grow within the city limits of Columbus. I'm sure I could find some in Washington and Monroe Counties without too much trouble. Be sure to ask the landowners' permission before gathering ramps on their land. (**Note:** Not long after this article was written, I found a ramp patch in Monroe County and I was shown another one in Washington County.)

March 9, 1981 –

"A country with no regard for its past will have little worth remembering in the future." These words, spoken by Abraham Lincoln, are very true; and a significant portion of man's past in this country is tied strongly to the National Forests.

Like a great history book, the National Forests hold the story of more than 10,000 years of human occupation. Most of us know about the major historical events related to settlement by early French and English colonists, trappers, farmers, and loggers. But we seldom realize that over 99 percent of the record of human life in North America was made by people who did not leave a written record - the American Indians.

Without written records we must look for other evidence of the way humans lived in the past, evidence existing on the ground in the form of prehistoric and historic archaeological objects and sites - the physical remains of human behavior. These cultural resources include rock shelters, campsites, petroglyphs, old buildings, pottery, arrow points, stone tools, and historic farmsteads, to name only a few.

Archaeologists can examine these remains and, with many new methods and techniques of recovery and analysis, interpret the past with great accuracy. But once a single object is carelessly removed from a prehistoric or early historic site, the record is damaged and incomplete - much as a book would be incomplete if words were erased or pages torn.

This evidence of the past is part of America's cultural heritage which belongs to all Americans. It is our legacy, left to us by peoples who lived in our land, met the challenge of the environment without modern technology, and left us a cultural heritage which extends back over 10,000 years. This heritage is a precious gift from generations of past Americans.

Before any ground disturbing activity takes place on National Forest land, we're required to make a reconnaissance survey for cultural artifacts. If anything significant is discovered, the activity will be halted until professional archaeologists can be consulted. They will then take necessary measures to protect the site.

The Forest Service manages these cultural resources in a manner which recognizes their significance and provides for their protection. The search for information about the history and prehistory of the National Forests is a continuing task. When the Forest Service completes its inventory of cultural resources, it will use the information to clarify the story of human occupation in these areas.

Locally we have many examples of cultural resources. The rock shelters, or rock houses, that are found throughout the hills provided shelter for prehistoric peoples for thousands of years. The old covered bridges in Monroe and Washington counties are unique and treasured links with the past. Several of the old iron furnaces from the 1800's still stand, such as Vinton Furnace and Vesuvius Furnace near Ironton. There are many abandoned cemeteries and mills throughout southeastern Ohio, too. And of course Indian arrowheads are somewhat common in the area, especially in the broad valleys along the Ohio River and its larger tributaries.

Helping to preserve America's heritage is one of the goals of the Forest Service. You can help preserve America's cultural heritage by leaving archaeological and historical remains undisturbed, encouraging others to do the same, and reporting your discoveries to Forest Service personnel. Collecting artifacts or disturbing sites on National Forest land without written permission is prohibited under terms of the Federal Antiquities Act of 1906 and the Archaeological Resources Protection Act of 1979.

To follow Abraham Lincoln's thinking -- preserving our cultural past may well help us to better plan, prepare for, and understand the future.

March 16, 1981 –

On Thursday, March 26 Dr. Bob Alrutz of the Ohio Environmental Council and Mrs. Marilyn Ortt of Marietta will be hosting a workshop to promote public participation in environmental policy making matters. The meeting will be held at 7:30 p.m. in Thomas Hall at Marietta College.

The meeting will focus around the upcoming Land Management Planning process for the Wayne National Forest. The planning process will actually begin sometime this Fall and will hopefully be completed by 1983. This Wayne National Forest Plan will give direction for our management activities over the next 10 years. So, anyone interested in the Wayne National Forest should get involved in helping prepare the Land Management Plan.

It's sometimes difficult to get all concerned parties involved in a process like this. Usually the more vocal groups and individuals will let you know what they think, but the majority of affected citizens remain silent. In developing the Wayne Plan, we want the help and involvement of all those people who are using, or are interested in, the National Forest.

Back to the meeting. It won't be a gripe session or a shouting match of some kind. It will be an orderly, structured, 2-hour meeting. The objectives of the meeting are:

1)   To provide information about the Wayne National Forest. There will be a slide program and then a chance to meet some of the people who work on the Forest.

2)   To provide information about Land Management Planning. Understanding the process will help you to help us develop an effective 10 year plan.

3)   To start to identify major issues, which should be resolved in the Wayne Plan. We'll break up into small working groups for this part.

Hunters, hikers, fishermen, land owners, timber cutters, bird-watchers, and others ---- if you have an interest in the Wayne National Forest, you're invited to attend the meeting on March 26. If you can't make it at this time, however, don't worry. There will be other chances for you to get involved this Fall and Winter when the planning process actually begins.

Over the past couple of weeks I've had the chance to present programs about Forest Management to three separate organizations --the Churchtown 4-H Club, Marietta College's Outdoor Recreation class, and the Marietta Women's Club. All three groups were very knowledgeable and interested in the Wayne National Forest. I'd like to thank Ken Pottmeyer's 4-H group; Debbie Lazorik and her class at Marietta College; and Mrs. Adkins, Mrs. Copeland, Mrs. Beckwith, Mrs. Oberholzer and all the ladies of the Women's Club for their interest in the Wayne National Forest. We're very busy now, and it's impossible to speak to every group and organization, but if you let us know far enough in advance we can work something out to schedule a presentation.

RANGER'S NOTEBOOK - The National Forest Management Act, passed by Congress in 1976, requires each National Forest in the country to prepare a Land Management Plan, which outlines activities for the

Forest over the next 10 years. All Plans must be completed no later than 1985. The Wayne National Forest Plan is scheduled for completion in 1983.

March 23, 1981 -

Forestry in the United States is a relatively new profession when compared to other countries, especially certain European countries. Forestry didn't really begin to take shape here until the early 1900's. In spite of this fact, rules and regulations pertaining to Forestry have been with us since the days of our first colonists.

From time to time I'll provide short historical sketches about these early days in American Forestry.

Today - The Colonial Period (1600-1777).

When the earliest settlers landed on American shores, forests covered nearly all the land from the eastern seaboard to the Great Plains. Wood was abundant and free for the taking. The colonial period was characterized by a gradual pushing back of the forests to make room for settlement.

Because transportation facilities were poor, local wood shortages sometimes arose near the larger towns, and these occasionally led to restrictions on cutting. But most people felt, in the words of Gifford Pinchot, that "the thing to do with the Forest was to get rid of it".

Here are some of the earliest laws on record:

1626 - Plymouth Colony passed an ordinance prohibiting cutting timber on colony lands without official consent.

1681 - William Penn's ordinance for the Pennsylvania colony required that, in clearing land, settlers leave 1 acre in trees for every 5 acres cleared. This provision wasn't enforced for very long.

1691 - Massachusetts colony charter reserved to the King, to provide masts for the British Navy, all white pine trees 2 feet thick or more (at one foot above the ground) growing on land not previously granted to a private person. Later, similar provisions applied from Maine to New Jersey. Violators were tried in admiralty courts.

1710 - The first community forest in the United States was established at Newington, New Hampshire. A 110-acre forest owned by the town has yielded continuing benefits to the community for more than two centuries, helping to build the village church, parsonage, town hall, and library; furnishing planks for bridges; and fuel to heat public buildings.

1728 - British Navigation Acts prohibited the colonies from shipping pitch, tar, and crude gum direct to foreign countries. Measures for the regulation of the naval stores industry and for the payment of bounties were introduced by the Royal Governor of North Carolina.

1760 - Another of America's earliest community forests was established at Danville, New Hampshire. A committee was appointed to manage the town's 75-acre woodland "to keep the parson warm." Over the years the forest has yielded some $10,000 worth of products.

1777 - North Carolina law prohibited unlawful firing of woods and declared that forest fires are extremely destructive to the soil.

Though forests were generally considered a "hindrance" to early colonists, some people realized the long-range value of protecting and managing our forest reserves.

<u>RANGER'S NOTEBOOK</u> - The U.S. Forest Service put out a film during our Bicentennial Year, titled "Roots of a Nation". The movie traces how trees and forests have been vital to the development of this country. If you contact us far enough ahead of time, we can usually arrange to show this movie to groups.

March 30, 1981 -

With the coming of Spring each person looks forward to the beautiful "rebirth" of all the plants and animals around us. The days get longer. Temperatures get warmer. It's time to start thinking about farms and gardens. Soon we'll see leaves on trees and wildflowers emerging from the forest floor. Fishermen are beginning to get their rods and reels ready.

As a forester it's very wonderful time of year for me. But also, as a forester it's a time of year that can cause me great worry. You see, as it gets warmer, and drier, and the winds pick up, last Fall's leaves dry out. Then presto, the stage is set for the return of one of the greatest enemies a forest knows -- uncontrolled wildfire!

In recent years we've come to realize that controlled fires can be beneficial tools for the forester -- to improve wildlife habitat, to prepare sites for tree planting, to reduce fire hazards, etc. Still, uncontrolled fires can cause many problems.

Severe fires can destroy trees (even large ones), kill wildlife and destroy their homes, burn up barns and houses, and even take human lives. Even the lesser fires which burn close to the surface can cause damage to the forest. By scorching the bases of the large trees, fires can open wounds through which disease enters. This will lower the value of the lumber sawn later, destroy wood faster than it grows, and increase the likelihood that the trees will be broken by the wind. When trees become weakened, insects can successfully attack and kill them.

Young trees can be killed outright. Repeated burns consume the litter on the forest floor, which drastically affects the fertility of the soil. Soil runoff and ashes also do harm to our creeks and streams.

Each year in this country we can expect over 100,000 fires that burn between 3 and 4 million acres. Of these fires, 9 out of 10 are caused by human carelessness or are set deliberately. In the western United States many fires are caused by lightning; but in the East lightning fires are few and far between.

Over $350 million dollars are spent each year as a direct result of forest fires. This is for fire prevention, fire detection, firefighting, and rehabilitation of burned areas. The public pays the bill in higher taxes and higher prices for forest products. Tremendous savings could be made if man-caused fires were prevented.

Careful use of matches, cigarettes, and campfires is a must. When extinguishing fires, make sure they are completely out before leaving. Don't burn on dry, windy days. Fire danger is high at these times, and a fire can escape rapidly. Also, keep in mind that if your fire escapes, you are liable for the costs of firefighting and for property damage to your neighbors.

Burning is generally safer after 4:00 p.m. In the evening there is usually less wind, higher humidity, and cooler temperatures, thus making it a safer time to burn than mid-day.

In addition to clearing a safe place to burn and checking the weather, be sure to have fire fighting tools ready if needed. Always have plenty of help available, too. And remember, stay with the fire until it is out -- dead out!

Fire is a tool that helps us in many ways, if we just use it wisely and treat it with respect.

RANGER'S NOTEBOOK -

In the Fall of 1871, the Peshtigo forest fire in Wisconsin burned over 1 million acres (including the entire town of Peshtigo) and caused the deaths of 1500 persons. The heat was so severe that dead fish floated on the rivers and birds were burned in flight and fell to the ground.

April 6, 1981 -

I've been asked several questions over the past few weeks concerning the payments we make to those counties having

National Forest lands within their boundaries. There are some misunderstandings about these payments that I'll attempt to clear up.

Starting in 1908, counties in the Eastern United States having National Forest lands within their boundaries began receiving money from what is known as "the 25% fund." This meant that 25% of the forest receipts from timber sales, special use permits, recreation fees, grazing fees, mineral leases, etc. were returned to the counties for their use. The money could be used only for school and road programs. The total receipts were added up, and then distributed according to the percentage of the entire National Forest that was contained by each county. For example, if Washington County contained 16% of the Wayne National Forest, then each year 16% of the returned money would go to Washington County.

This worked out very well for counties in certain states where large volumes of timber were sold or where large recreation areas generated a lot of income for the National Forest. However, in Ohio timber sales are relatively small and not of real high value. Other income, such as from recreation campgrounds, is also low compared to other National Forests. Congress, realizing an unequal situation existed between states, passed a law in 1976 to somewhat remedy the problem. The law, known as the "Payment in Lieu of Taxes" law (PILT), guaranteed that at least 75¢ per acre would be returned to counties having National Forest lands. This meant a large increase in money going to the eleven Ohio Counties of the Wayne National Forest.

Let's look at some figures.:

During the 10-year period prior to 1977 when the new law took effect, the per acre return to counties ranged from as low as 6¢ per acre to as high as 19¢ per acre. In 1977 the payments jumped to 85¢ per acre; 93¢ in 1978; 85¢ in 1979; and about 81¢ per acre in 1980. There's still some variation from year to year depending on timber sales, etc., but the minimum is 75¢ per acre.

One important feature of the new PILT payment is that the money can be used for any governmental purpose. However, most counties in the Eastern United States still use the money for schools and roads.

Lawrence County, downriver at Ironton, has the most acres of Wayne National Forest land of the eleven counties. It contains 54,450 acres of National Forest land. Washington County is in second place with 29,367 acres and Monroe County is fifth with 14,851 acres. The bottom two counties are Vinton and Jackson, with just a few hundred acres each.

Washington County received $24,158 in 1980 and Monroe County received $12,142. The entire eleven-county area received almost $150,000. In some counties the PILT payments are higher than the tax receipts would be if the land was in private ownership. In other counties, because of reassessments, the PILT payments may be lower. In either case the payments are fairly close to private tax rates for hilly, forested land.

So, although it's technically correct that the National Forest land isn't taxed, there are payments made to the counties to compensate for this.

If you have any questions please stop by our office in Reno or call 373-9055.

April 13, 1981 -

When grouse hunting season is over at the end of each February, most hunters clean their guns and store them until the following Fall. Out come their rods and reels, and fishing season begins. But as March and April come and go, there is a special group for whom the "true" hunting season will soon begin -- turkey hunters.

The wild turkey gobbler (male) is probably the most difficult game animal to hunt in the eastern United States. From personal experience I can attest to the fact that it takes many hours, even days, of scouting, preparation, and hunting to have even a reasonable chance of success. Taking nothing away from deer and grouse hunters, it is widely recognized that the measure of an outdoorsman and hunter lies in his ability to stalk the wild turkey. I don't rate very high on the list, either. Because whether I'm just trying to catch sight of a turkey, take a photograph of one, or am hunting for one, I usually strike out. But that's the challenge that the wily and cunning wild turkey presents.

The turkey's keenest sense is its eyesight. If you're in pursuit of wild turkey, I strongly suggest wearing camouflage clothing. I've often heard it said that "a deer treats every man in the woods as if he were a stump, while a turkey treats every stump in the woods as though it were a man." Enough said. Turkeys are cagey!

Two of our local experts on wild turkeys are Clifford Winstanley, State Game Protector, and Darrell Cline, local Chapter President of the Wild Turkey Federation - - a group dedicated to the expansion and protection of wild turkey habitat.

Clifford says there seem to be more turkeys around this year than the last few years. "The relatively mild winter and spring also brings hope for a good hatch this year," he said. "Hunting pressure in this area is light compared to other areas, such as Hocking and Vinton Counties. I wouldn't expect more than 25-35 hunters this spring in eastern Washington County and southern Monroe County," Winstanley told me.

Clifford said most of our turkeys are located in Grandview, Independence, and Ludlow Townships. The season this year runs from Monday, April 27 through Saturday, May 2 and from Monday, May 4 through

Saturday, May 9. Hunters may be in the woods from $^1/_2$ hour before sunrise until 12:00 noon. If you bag a turkey it must be checked in by 2:00 p.m. on the same day you kill it. The local checking station is the Amoco Service Station in New Matamoras. Winstanley recalled that only about 8 turkeys were killed in this area last year. Maybe you'll be one of the lucky hunters.

Darrell Cline, a former employee of the Wayne National Forest, put together the following thoughts on the wild turkey in southeastern Ohio. I'm sure you'll enjoy his insight -----

The early morning gray gradually gives way to a rosy glow in the East. White, pink and purple trilliums dot the leaf-covered forest floor. The inevitable bird songs seem to assist the sun higher in the eastern sky, as two whippoorwills trade songs, and in the distance a barred owl hoots his "who cooks-for you?" greeting. Amid all this we're treated to the spine-tingling gobble of a wild turkey, and then we're sure the magic hour for all wild turkey enthusiasts has arrived.

Only 25 years ago the call of the wild turkey could not be heard in the State of Ohio. Now it's a common occurrence to see and hear wild turkeys in more than 25 of the State's 88 counties. The majority of these counties with wild turkey populations are located in the southern part of Ohio, which contains the largest portion of the State's forested land. The return of the wild turkey to Ohio is a success story made possible by the Ohio Division of Wildlife and the U.S. Forest Service.

The native wild turkey was eliminated in Ohio when its range was destroyed by the vast, intensive lumbering and farming operations which spread across the state in the last century. The last record of a turkey being shot was in 1904 in Adams County.

The early depletion of much soil, water, timber and known mineral resources in Ohio's southern hills resulted in abandoned farms, failing industries, and a migration of people looking for jobs elsewhere. A few of the scars of misuse are being healed by nature and in some cases aided by man.

As the scalped and pastured hill land was once again permitted to grow trees, there was an increase in such forest animals as ruffed grouse and white-tailed deer. Wildlife biologists recognized that the forested areas were approaching the conditions required for wild turkey range.

The Ohio Division of Wildlife initiated a program to reintroduce the wild turkey. Forest areas selected for stocking were chosen primarily on the basis of size, 9,000 acres being the minimum. Two of the areas selected were located in the Wayne National Forest. One was on the Ironton District of the Forest in southern Ohio and the other was on the Muskingum Unit of the Athens Ranger District, and is locally known as the Irish-Jackson Run Wild Turkey Management Area.

Wild turkeys trapped in other states were received and stocked in 1956. Evaluation of this method of reintroduction has proven successful. On Sept. 2, 1960, two adult gobblers were live-trapped, the first record of such an accomplishment in Ohio. Since that time many turkeys have been trapped and transplanted to additional areas considered by the biologists to contain suitable wild turkey habitat.

Wildlife biologists kept close surveillance on the wild turkey flocks, and with yearly increases detected, it was decided that the population had reached a point to where surplus gobblers could be harvested in the spring of 1966. Five hundred permits were issued for 14 counties in 1966, and twelve wild gobblers were taken. Since that time the wild turkey population has steadily increased, and the Division of Wildlife has increased the number of permits to allow for harvest each year of surplus gobblers. In 1980 a total of 2,097 permits were issued for hunting in 20 counties. There were 387 gobblers harvested, bringing the total since 1966 to 1,575. Ohio's 1981 season will begin April 27th and end May 9th. Another record harvest is indicated, if the weather is suitable.

Wild turkeys being polygamous allows for the hunting of gobblers in the Spring after hens have commenced their incubation period which takes 28 days. The average clutch of eggs is 11 and the chicks can fly at 2 weeks of age. The primary food of the chicks is insects, and as they mature their typical foods are grass seeds, dogwood fruit, acorns, beechnuts, green leaves, tubers, fruits, and roots of many plants.

I could go on endlessly writing about this grand bird that Benjamin Franklin suggested becoming America's National symbol, and which once again echoes its booming gobble from hill to hill in the Buckeye State.

The Ohio Division of Wildlife and the U.S. Forest Service are to be commended for the amazing goal they have achieved. They have taken the wildest "critter" in North America, put it in a state with almost 11 million people and very limited range, protected it, and seen it become an established resident. The wild turkey is providing a unique aesthetic and cultural value, as well as a hunting recreational value, to the citizens of Ohio.

April 20, 1981 -

Spring is a wonderful time in southeastern Ohio. The hills and valleys seem to come alive after their long winter's rest. Though Fall is my favorite season of the year, there is something about Spring that refreshes everyone's spirit.

In the hills we have a variety of native trees that burst into early color, often even before Winter is quite over. These colorful "eye pleasers" include redbud, dogwood, pin cherry, red maple, and serviceberry.

The serviceberry, or "sarvus" tree, is one of the most beautiful of our native trees. It is among the earliest of our spring-blooming woody plants, with the pretty white flowers blooming soon after the first warm weather. The white blossoms dot the landscape in late March or early April and often last for over a month. By summertime the "sarvus" produces fruit, which is edible, and is eaten by birds, wild animals, and people. The fruit, which resembles little apples, makes excellent jelly.

There is an old mountain tale which explains how the serviceberry got its name. Back in the early days of settling the Appalachian Mountains, families would settle in certain hollows and pretty much live and die there. Most major hollows had their own church, schoolhouse, and maybe a small general store. Many people only went into town a couple times a year. Circuit preachers generally made the "rounds" giving church services over a wide area. Generally these services were given in the Spring, Summer, and Fall, because in the old days Winter travel was either difficult or impossible in most places.

So, if there were any deaths during the Winter months, there was no preacher available to perform the funeral. Since the mountains stay fairly cold all Winter long, there was no problem storing the bodies in a cold place until the Spring thaw, at which time the circuit preacher was able to start back on his "rounds" giving several burial services or "sarvuses". The ground was thawed enough, too, so that digging a grave was no problem. Well, normally by the time the preacher gave his first burial "sarvus" each Spring, the pretty, white tree was beginning to bloom, hence the name serviceberry or sarvus.

I first heard this story from a relative of mine and I'm fairly certain there's some truth to it. There are many, many common names throughout our area which originated like the serviceberry---by association with some common event or happening.

RANGER'S NOTEBOOK - You'll hear nurserymen and botanists refer to the serviceberry as

Amelanchier arborea. By using this "scientific name" there is no confusion with other species, thus the scientists know exactly which tree they're talking about. By comparison, there are often many, many common or local names for the same tree. This can be confusing when going to a different area. The serviceberry, for instance, is also called sarvus, Juneberry, downy serviceberry, mountain sarvus, and shad bush, depending on where you live. Six names for the same tree! Definitely this could be confusing for a scientist or botanist, so they stick with Amelanchier arborea no matter where they live or work.

April 27, 1981 -

When people talk about colorful Spring trees and beautiful ornamental trees, they generally speak of dogwood, redbud, serviceberry or other such common beauties. However, when you come to think about it, there's one tree that offers as much year-round color to the forest as any other species. It's the often overlooked red maple.

As Spring comes forth to the mountains, part of the early color is brought on by the red maple, as the reddish flowers emerge onto the bare limbs. Where there are several red maples growing together, the

Spring color is as beautiful as the serviceberry or dogwood.

The Fall leaves of the red maple turn a brilliant scarlet, and are among the prettiest in the woods. The bark of the red maple is a smooth gray color on the younger trees. When growing in clumps, these trees are very pretty, offering a pleasing contrast to the rough bark of the oaks and pines.

The red maple grows throughout eastern North America and is perhaps our most widely spread tree. It is found in Canada, as well as southern Florida, which indicates the tree adapts well to various growing conditions.

The wing-like seeds of the red maple are blown for quite long distances, which enables the species to seed-in over quite an area. Also, when the larger trees are cut, the stumps produce clusters of fast-growing sprouts which can almost dominate certain sites.

Red maple is one of those trees that isn't particularly loved by anyone, but in truth is one of our most abundant and important species. It grows fast and vigorously, but isn't especially valuable as a timber tree. Its wood is somewhat soft and weak, and is sold as "soft maple". (The sugar maple is a more valuable timber tree and is sold as "hard maple"). Red maple timber commonly goes into cheaper furniture, crates, pallets, pulpwood, etc. The wood is often defective, and many of the trees over 20 inches in diameter are culls. Red maple is very susceptible to wounds and rot. Because of its thin bark it can be killed by ground fires.

Red maple has been planted in several towns and cities as an ornamental and shade tree. It doesn't grow extremely large and has an attractive, tight crown.

As a food for wildlife, the red maple is excellent. Browsing animals, such as deer, love to eat the tender sprouts (which are also red); squirrels and chipmunks feed on the seeds; and several birds, including grouse, find the buds a tasty treat.

The red maple may not be our most important timber tree; it may not be the preferred food for all wildlife species; and you may have a tree you think is more colorful. But considering its many qualities and its wide range, it is definitely one of our most valuable all-around tree species.

May 11, 1981 -

The Wayne National Forest is one of 155 National Forests in this country, which are administered by the U.S. Forest Service. The Forest Service is part of the Department of Agriculture. Nationally there are nine separate Forest Service "Regions," Ohio being in the Eastern Region.

A sister forest to the Wayne is the Hoosier National Forest in Indiana. Because both of these Forests are relatively small, they have been combined into one administrative unit and are referred to as the "Wayne-Hoosier National Forests."

The Forest Supervisor for these Forests is Harold Godlevske, and he maintains his administrative offices in Bedford, Indiana. His assistant, Bjorn Dahl, is Deputy Forest Supervisor for the Wayne-Hoosier. Together, these two men are responsible for the administration of the Forest, including policy decisions, personnel matters, coordination with other agencies and outside groups, and setting direction for managing the Forests' resources. Of course their job is a very complex one, and they have a large staff in Bedford to assist them. Their staff includes specialists in such areas as Recreation, Timber, Engineering, Minerals, Administrative Services, Lands, Wildlife, and Fire, as well as others.

The Wayne-Hoosier National Forests are further broken down into Ranger Districts, two in each state --- - Brownstown and Tell City in Indiana; Ironton and Athens in Ohio. The management of these four Districts is handled by a District Ranger, who in turn has a workforce of people to carry out the various jobs such as tree planting, operating recreation areas, soil and watershed restoration, timber management, coordinating mineral activities, etc.

As pointed out in previous columns, the Marietta Unit is part of the Athens Ranger District, administered by District Ranger Bob Joens. Because of the distance from Athens to Washington and Monroe Counties, we maintain the Marietta (Reno) office with a supervisory forester and staff in order to better serve the public.

I hope this makes it more clear how the Wayne-Hoosier National Forests are organized, and how Marietta and Athens fit into the total picture. If you have questions, please stop by our office on Rt. 7 in Reno or give us a call at 373-9055.

On another topic --- I had a very enjoyable evening a couple of weeks ago when I attended the Vocational Banquet at Frontier High School. The Banquet was sponsored by the Future Farmers of America (FFA), Future Homemakers of America (FHA), and the Office Education Association (OEA). It was put on totally by student members of these three groups, and they did a fine job.

I attended as a guest of Calvin Martin, a teacher at Frontier who is advisor to the FFA group. I've been helping Calvin and the FFA group locate some tree species on the

Wayne National Forest that can be transplanted into their outdoor "Land Laboratory," located just below the High School on the Ohio River bank. They have an excellent facility there, which they use for outdoor projects such as wildlife habitat improvement and tree identification.

Calvin has worked extensively with Wildlife Biologist Mike Budzik of the Ohio Department of Natural Resources, to develop a master plan for managing several acres between the football field and the river. Calvin and his students have worked very hard to carry out many of the projects in the master plan.

I was up there one day recently to take a look at their various tree species, and we made a list of the ones they needed in order to have a more complete representation of local trees. We have either gotten or will be getting a couple different types of hickories, 2 or 3 species of oaks, a honey locust, sugar maple, Ohio buckeye, and a Kentucky coffeetree. We've located some small saplings of these trees. The students will dig them, transplant them, and they'll become the newest residents of Frontier's Land Laboratory. They've transplanted a few this Spring, but most will probably have to wait until next February or March when chances for successful transplanting will be better.

Frontier's "Land Lab" is a tribute to the support by the administration at the High School and to the care and efforts of Calvin Martin and his Vo-Ag students. At the High School level, it's as fine an outdoor facility as you'll find anywhere.

May 18, 1981 -

Forest roads are a familiar sight to anyone visiting the Wayne National Forest. The roads are part of a transportation system that is needed in order to provide access for Forest users and Forest managers. Roads are used for a variety of activities ranging from timber hauling and sightseeing to recreation area access and fire control purposes.

The standard of these roads on the National Forest varies according to the type of use each one receives. For instance, there are high-standard, paved roads like in our developed picnic and camping areas, and on the other end of the scale there are short, temporary roads that are used to bring logs to a central landing for loading and hauling by log trucks.

The number of roads needed in a Forest also varies according to management activities and use patterns. And, of course, some people always think we should have more roads, while others think we should have fewer roads.

Despite differences of opinion as to the standard of road needed and how many there should be, two facts stand out. First, intensive, multiple-use, forest management requires a certain number of roads; and second, all road construction and maintenance projects bring the potential for soil erosion and stream sedimentation.

The percentage of soil erosion occurring in the United States as a result of forest management activities is a very small percentage of the total. Most soil erosion comes from farming, followed by things such as runoff from housing developments and shopping centers, new construction, the highway system throughout the country, etc. However, this doesn't mean that soil and water considerations are unimportant in forest management. They're very important indeed!

The main cause of soil erosion and stream siltation in forestry-related work is from roads. One common misconception is that clear-cutting causes soil erosion. This is totally false. Soil must be bared for erosion to occur, and cutting a tree doesn't bare any soil. The road built to remove the trees can, however, cause soil erosion.

Since roads offer the greatest potential for soil erosion in forest management, and since we know that some roads are going to be necessary, we must concentrate our soil and water protection efforts on proper road location, construction, and maintenance.

These are some of the items that we consider when planning our roads:

1) Stay away from unstable soils, steep slopes and springs or wet, boggy areas.

2) Locate roads as far away from streams as possible.

3) If stream crossings are necessary, cross at right angles using culverts or bridges; gravel approaches as necessary.

4) Limit roads to the minimum mileage needed.

5) Quickly reseed disturbed soils along road banks, or whenever roads will be closed permanently.

6) Leave buffer strips of vegetation between roads and streams, which will serve as sediment traps.

7) Plan regular maintenance on permanent roads.

8) Adequate surfacing, such as gravel on primary logging roads, is a must.

9) Since many roads aren't constructed for all-weather use, close those during off-season periods.

A properly located, constructed, and maintained forest road will result in few environmental problems, and is likely to have lower maintenance costs in the long run.

RANGER'S NOTEBOOK –

Timber has played a major role in the growth and development of the United States. It has been estimated that 2,400,000 million board feet of lumber were cut between 1776 and World War II, enough to build 52,000,000 urban homes, 12,000,000 farmhouses, 2,000,000 schools and libraries, 650,000 churches, and 450,000 factories.

June 1, 1981 –

Miscellaneous Notes

We just recently received the revised and updated maps of the Wayne National Forest. The Forest is divided into three units-Athens, Marietta, and Ironton. Each unit is mapped separately and the cost is $1.00 per map.

These new maps are designated as Forest Service Class A maps and were compiled from U.S. Geological Survey Quadrangles. The scale of the maps is $1/_2$ inch equals one mile and revisions are accurate through at least 1975.

National Forest land is shown on the maps in green color on a white background. The mapped area outside the National Forest is shown in light yellow color.

Maps can be purchased by stopping in the office on Rt. 7 in Reno or by writing to:

Wayne National Forest

Rt. 1

Marietta, Ohio 45750

Map purchases can be by cash, check, or money order. Checks or money orders must be made payable to: Forest Service--USDA.

As with any publication, errors will be detected. A correction map will be maintained for the next revision, and we will appreciate the reporting of any errors you might find to our office.

*There is an area on the Shawnee National Forest in southern Illinois that has a unique distinction. They close a portion of the Forest, including a road, twice a year in order to protect migrating snakes.

*Spring rains have decreased the chances of a second successive dry summer across much of the eastern half of the United States. However, a long-term and widespread moisture deficit persists in the subsoil, and more rains will be needed before the drought is completely over. In the West, the most serious drought area seems to be Colorado.

*An interesting note about John Muir, one of this country's earliest naturalists. -- As a child he grew up in the home of his preacher-farmer Dad. By the time he became a teenager he had memorized the entire New Testament of the Bible and much of the Old Testament. He also spent a lot of time studying French, Latin, and other languages. Following an accident that threatened his sight, Muir vowed that, if he got well, he would never again study the works of men, only the works of God. He then became a self-taught geologist and one of the foremost naturalists of all time. Muir probably influenced the American movement to preserve unspoiled areas for National Parks as much as Teddy Roosevelt and Gifford Pinchot influenced the movement to establish National Forests.

*The eruption of Mount St. Helens last year severely hurt the elk population in that area. Approximately 2,000 elk were killed during and immediately after the May 18, 1980 eruption, while around 4,000 elk survived. According to the Washington Wildlife Commission, that area was prime elk habitat. Some large elk herds have been discovered moving back into the blasted area, which is covered by mudflows and ash. They are surviving by eating the new emerging grasses and also the tree seedlings which were planted by the Forest Service and the Soil Conservation Service.

June 8, 1981 -

The local oil and gas activity sure is something! It seems as though every other vehicle you pass on the roads is related to the oil and gas industry. We're in the midst of quite a flurry around here. All the activity definitely stimulates the area by putting money into the local economy and by creating jobs for local people.

Now, there are some trade-offs to be made, because with all good things there comes a little bad. Primarily here, we're talking about the heavy wear and tear on our local roads and bridges caused by the large trucks. Most oil and gas operators feel some responsibility for road maintenance and contribute their fair share. Others don't and this is where problems come in. Recent indications are, however, that the operators, Township Trustees, County officials, and concerned citizens will be working together to improve road conditions. Let's hope things work out.

We're often asked about all the drilling that's occurring on the Wayne National Forest and why we allow it. The main reason is that we do <u>not</u> own the mineral rights under most of the surface in Monroe and Washington Counties. The minerals are privately owned, and the owner of the subsurface has the right to go in and extract his property. (I'm just estimating, but I believe the government owns the minerals on only 10% of the land in these two counties). So there's the reason - the minerals are privately owned.

The mineral status beneath the Wayne National Forest falls into 3 categories. The <u>first</u> is where the United States owns the minerals, and as I indicated, this is only 10% (or less). The second category is reserved mineral rights. This came about when someone sold the government a tract of land, but they reserved the mineral rights for themselves. The mineral owners are free to develop their minerals, but they must comply with State laws and some Forest Service requirements, such as obtaining a permit from us, posting a bond, and working with us to find the most suitable locations. Still, they own the minerals, and have the right to develop them. The third category is outstanding mineral rights, where the person who sold us a tract of land did not own the minerals. They had already been separated from the surface by previous owners. In these cases the operators must comply only with State laws, but almost every operator is attempting to work with us too, particularly in site selection. Our goal in these instances is not to hinder or harass anyone from the legal exercise of their rights, but to minimize the adverse impacts on the Wayne National Forest. National Forests belong to all citizens, and these citizens expect us to manage and protect the Forest as well as we can.

It's quite a job to keep track of everything occurring on the Wayne National Forest, but we do our best. Last year, Washington County led the State in number of wells drilled with over 1,000. (Someone told me this was close to tops in the whole country, also). They're projecting 1,000 or more new wells in Washington County for the next couple of years, too. The Monroe County activity is not this heavy, but it is steadily increasing. So we know that for the foreseeable future we'll be quite busy trying to minimize the impacts of all this drilling, and trying to coordinate it with all our other activities, such as recreation, wildlife management, timber management etc.

Decreasing our dependence on foreign oil and finding new supplies of natural gas are both helping to solve our energy problems. Southeastern Ohio seems to be doing its part. If you have any questions, don't hesitate to call (373-9055), or stop by our office in Reno.

June 15, 1981 –

Camping season is here! Hiking, too, if only the rain would quit for a while. It's fun to get into the outdoors and enjoy yourself each Spring and Summer. Here are some things you might want to consider:

- If you're not camping in a mobile trailer, your tent is probably your most important piece of gear. It should be clean, provide ample space for everyone, be waterproof, and be flame-resistant.

- If you're hiking or backpacking to a new location each night, you may wish to use one of the newer, lighter tents. Even a few pounds of extra weight can be a hindrance on long hikes.

- The tent should be easy to set up and be of durable construction. It should have adequate ventilation and a mosquito net on the door.

- Before storing your tent after the trip clean it out thoroughly, repair any holes, wash off all dirt and let it dry completely. Then store it in a dry place.

- If hiking, take plenty of high energy foods and water. However, don't over-estimate your food needs. That would be extra weight. Freeze-dried foods are very light to carry, and actually, they don't taste too bad.

- If you're camping and have coolers, dry ice will last longer than regular ice. Wrap it in newspaper to keep it from touching your cooler or your skin. It can burn, so be careful!

- Open your cooler as little as possible. Each time you open it, you lose some of the cold air. When I worked in the Boundary Waters Canoe Area in northern Minnesota, I would normally take two coolers with me on camping or canoeing trips. One contained everything that didn't need refrigeration or that would be used in the first 2-3 days. The other cooler was well insulated and contained all frozen foods. By not opening that cooler until sometimes on the 4th day out, we often kept fresh meat, milk, etc., unspoiled for 6 or 7 days. (Of course we were travelling by canoe; if you're walking, I'd still suggest freeze-dried foods. Just be sure to boil that water before adding it to the packages).

- If you're cooking out, don't use an old refrigerator shelf for your grill. Some of these were coated with cadmium and when heated give off a poison.

- When in the woods, don't throw your trash down. Burn it or carry it out with you. Obey all state and federal fire laws; be especially careful in the early Spring and late Fall.

- Always carry a first aid kit with you. Let someone know where you're going and when you'll return. Take some mosquito, chigger, tick, and bug repellant along. Make sure you can identify poison ivy. Stay away from it! There's no such thing as being "immune" to poison ivy.

These are only a few helpful hints to keep in mind when going hiking or camping. I'll list some others in a future column. If you have specific questions, please feel free to call us at 373-9055 or stop by the office on Route 7 in Reno. We hope you enjoy your hiking and camping trips.

June 22, 1981 -

Three or four weeks ago in one of my columns I ran a few general interest items on a variety of outdoor subjects. Several readers said they enjoyed that particular column and would like to see more of them in the future. I'll try to write a column like this every month or so. Here goes!

Bits and Pieces from the Great Outdoors

- Remember reading about the sinkholes that were occurring in Florida a few weeks ago? Well, a 40-year-old wood frame house remained intact when it settled in a giant sinkhole near Winter Haven. Other nearby buildings, including several of concrete-masonry construction, broke apart. A victory for wood!

-If you're planning to vacation out West this summer, keep this in mind: Several bubonic plague-infected rodents have been found in California and Nevada this year. In recent years other states in the West and Southwest have also reported this. Last fall, near Lake Tahoe, a woman died from the plague. I sure wouldn't cancel any trips, because catching the disease is not very likely, especially if you take precautions. The main precaution? Don't - I repeat, don't - pick up or touch any chipmunks, squirrels, etc. that seem to be sick or injured. Leave them alone and report it to the nearest authority.

-Another health hazard reported -- the caterpillar of the gypsy moth, if touched, can cause rashes, welts, and itching. The gypsy moth is found primarily in the East and Northeast, especially New England. Entomologists report that "caterpillar-itis" is much more widespread than most people think. There are several types of caterpillars that are considered poisonous to people. In general, those that are more colorful are more poisonous than those with less pronounced markings.

-How about a bear story? My parents are both from Pocahontas County in the mountains of eastern West Virginia. I was born there, too. So were a lot of bears. That area is one of the last strongholds in the East for the black bear. Periodic reports of bear sightings often come from other areas, including southeastern Ohio. Usually, most people scoff at these "sightings" and attribute them to being a large dog or something. Growing up where Ohio, West Virginia, and Kentucky meet, near Huntington, I often heard about such sightings. But they were never verified, and the last bear killed in that area had been many, many years previous. Now, however, we have some one-hundred percent, genuine proof of bears in southeastern Ohio. People in several counties have recently reported bear sightings. While most people were still laughing, one bear was treed near Zanesville and quite a few people got a look at him, including an Ohio DNR game biologist. The bear's path had been traced from where he had crossed the Ohio River near Pomeroy, travelled up toward Athens, close to Burr Oak Lake, and then on to the Zanesville area.

After coming down from the tree, the bear headed east and officers report he crossed the Ohio River back into West Virginia's northern Panhandle, heading full speed for Pennsylvania. Another bear was verified to have been spotted in Pike County, near Waverly, Ohio. Bear populations in West Virginia have been on the upswing in recent years, and since they travel over long distances, look for more reported sightings in southeastern Ohio. If your neighbor swears he saw a bear while on a Sunday afternoon drive, think twice before laughing at him. Till next time, so long.

July 6, 1981 -

Monday, July 13 marks the beginning of this summer's Youth Conservation Corps (YCC) Camp. Because of the uncertainty of funding, we didn't find out until mid-June that we would even be able to have a camp this year. But with some fast work, particularly by Ed Payne, we've gotten things organized and ready to go.

Ed has worked with the summer YCC program every year since 1971. (That was the year of the first Little Muskingum YCC Camp, which was also the first one in the state of Ohio). During the rest of the year, Ed works in the Monroe County school system. He has been both principal and teacher in the Switzerland of Ohio School District. His knowledge, experience, and teaching ability have been of great benefit to the Wayne National Forest, because not only is the YCC program a work experience, it is also a learning experience. Ten hours per week are devoted to environmental education. Over the last 10 years, approximately 800 campers have benefitted from YCC's unique blend of working and learning. (Not to mention earning a salary for a fun summer's worth of outdoor work).

Because of the funding difficulties, this year's program will be a little different from those of past years. In the past, up to 40 campers from all over the state actually lived at our permanent camp just south of Bloomfield. This year, however, the enrollees will live at home and report to work each morning just like a regular job. They'll still use the Bloomfield Camp as their base of operations though.

We'll have seven enrollees from all over Monroe and Washington counties attending the camp this summer. These "lucky seven" were chosen at random from a group of over 30 hopefuls. (I wish we had enough money to offer them all a job, but this year we just don't). The list includes kids from Sardis, Moss Run, Marietta, Whipple, and Wingett Run. We also keep a list of alternates in case someone drops out of the program.

Work is done under strict supervision with safety our foremost concern. Projects this year include: hiking trail maintenance, erosion control work, recreation area clean-up, constructing two portal signs along Route 7, and maintenance projects at the YCC Camp. The sign project will be a very interesting one, and the kids will be able to see the results of their work for years to come. One sign will go up above Newport, while the other one will go in near Fly. The large signs will be worded "Wayne National Forest."

You may see the group out working this summer. If you do, you'll know what they're doing. We're glad we have these seven enrollees working this summer. For without them, a lot of projects wouldn't be done.

YCC – Youngsters working, earning, and learning on the Wayne National Forest.

RANGER'S NOTEBOOK – The Youth Conservation Corps (YCC) is a federally funded program administered jointly by the Department of Agriculture and the Department of Interior in conjunction with several states. The State of Ohio has always had one of the best, and one of the largest, programs of any state. The Ohio Department of Natural Resources administers various state camps in addition to the one we host here at the Wayne National Forest.

July 13, 1981 -

Are you a hunter or fisherman? If so, whether you know it or not, you're helping to finance fish & wildlife management and restoration programs across the country.

The numbers of license holders in each State are used by the U.S. Fish and Wildlife Service - Department of the Interior in determining the amount of funds returned to the state. States can be reimbursed for up to 75% of the costs of approved restoration and management programs.

Americans who hunted and fished last year spent a record $418 million on licenses, tags, permits, and stamps. Income was up $45 million over 1979 figures.

The total number of hunting license holders in the United States was over 16 million, while fishing license holders numbered over 27 million. These figures don't fully reflect all hunters and anglers, however, because many persons are exempt from buying licenses. These include senior citizens, persons under 16 years of age, the handicapped, and certain military personnel; and many States don't require licenses for salt-water fishing.

According to the figures I saw, California led the nation in total fishing licenses issued, with over 5 million. Ohio was number 11 on the list with over 1 million licenses issued.

On the hunting license list, Pennsylvania was number one with over 2 million, while Ohio stood in 16th place with around 700,000 total licenses issued. Ohio is certainly one of the major states when it comes to fishing, hunting, and other outdoor activities.

*In recent years backpackers and hikers who drink from surface water sources have encountered increasing cases of intestinal trouble. One of the main causes is giardia lamblia protozoa. The best advice is to: 1) carry your water with you on short trips, or 2) always boil water you use along the trail.

*A lot of the coal produced in this country is exported abroad. The Washington Post reports that world demand for U.S. coal exports will double by 1990. Those exports are projected to rise to between 125 million and 150 million tons a year by then.

*Forty years ago a desert shrub was considered to be a good bet in helping meet this country's need for rubber. Over 30,000 acres were planted to guayule (pronounced wy-oo-lee) during World War II. However, the plants were burned when the war ended because Asian supplies of rubber returned and the rubber industry turned to synthetics. Now the reverse situation is occurring. With the turmoil in Southeast Asia, things are unpredictable there;

and because synthetic rubber uses petroleum, other alternatives are being looked at. Now the U.S. Department of Agriculture is planting 120 acres of 5 species of guayule for testing. An additional 80 acres will be planted this Fall. Plantings are in California, New Mexico, Arizona, and Texas.

*Do you collect post cards of places you visit during vacations? I don't really "collect" them, but I do save some of them. What this is leading up to is - get ready! - that if you collect post cards as a hobby, you're a deltiologist. No kidding, a deltiologist! All these years and I didn't even know. I guess they have a name for everything.

So long till next week; hope you enjoy the great outdoors and your.....Wayne National Forest.

August 3, 1981 -

The American Chestnut tree was at one time perhaps the most valuable and widespread tree growing in the Appalachian Mountains, occurring from Alabama and Georgia all the way to Maine. The tree was highly prized for its nuts, which mountain people were able to sell for a profit as well as use to supplement their own food supply. The nuts also were used and preferred by many species of wildlife; this was an important reason for the abundance of game in the mountains. As far as the wood itself, there were so many uses for it that I can't list them all. Some of these uses were split-rail fences, roof shingles, tools, telegraph poles, railroad ties, and furniture. Its resistance to rot and decay made it a very popular wood indeed. The long lasting nature of chestnut wood can still be seen by the firm, solid snags that remain in our forests today.

It was truly one of the worst natural tragedies of our time when the chestnut blight destroyed all the native American Chestnuts. The blight, which is caused by a fungus, was first noticed in the New York Zoological Garden in 1904. It was accidentally introduced there on some plants that came from Asia. Within about 40-45 years all the Chestnut trees in this country were dead. No trees survived from the large stands, which had individuals up to 100 feet tall and 3-5 feet in diameter. There are reports of trees which measured 13-15 feet in diameter.

Almost from the beginning of the blight's occurrence, scientists began searching for cures. Nothing was very successful. And to further complicate the problem, the blight found its way to Europe, where it devastated chestnut trees in Italy by the 1930's and France by the 1950's.

However, in recent years the blight in Italy seemed to have cured itself. Noticing this, a scientist in France began work to help nature's healing process speed up somewhat.

It seems that the fungus eventually weakens to a point where the tree can defeat it. And when weak fungus and strong fungus touch each other, they both seem to become weak, allowing the tree to recover. The blight in Italy is almost gone now and France is curing it at a fast rate. There are high hopes by scientists that this will happen in the United States in the near future. The trick will be to get the weak strain of fungus to spread naturally throughout our forests just as the first fungus did over a half century ago. This occurred faster in Europe because many of the chestnut trees grew in pure stands and groves, whereas in this country the chestnut was very widespread and grew in mixed stands with many other tree species. But scientists are very hopeful that, with themselves speeding up the process as best they can, nature will take care of the blight in the near future.

There are at least two major research centers, one in Connecticut and one in West Virginia, which are working almost full-time on the problem of the chestnut blight. Maybe within our lifetimes the beautiful and valuable chestnut will once again take its rightful place in our mountain forests.

RANGER'S NOTEBOOK - Chestnut blight kills the tree, but does not affect the root system. Therefore, chestnut sprouts are abundant in all of the Eastern mountain forests, including here in southeastern Ohio.

This is because the American chestnut is one of the most prolific sprouters of any tree. However, by the time these small trees reach big enough size to bear nuts, the blight kills them back and the re-sprouting process starts again.

August 10, 1981 -

As of September 1st we'll be located in a new building, two doors up from our present location. Our new office will be the one which First Colony recently moved out of. Our mailing address will remain the same (Rt. 1 Marietta) and we hope that since we're moving just a short distance, there won't be any inconvenience to the public. We'll have a temporary sign put up on Rt. 7 until we're able to have a new one made. If for some reason you can't locate the new office, our phone number remains the same - 373-9055.

This new location gives us a little more room, but most importantly it gives us a workshop area where we can perform minor maintenance and repair work. We didn't have workshop space at our old location.

All moves are a little hectic, but the short distance involved should minimize any confusion. When we're finished, I think we'll be better able to serve the public.

Stop by to see us, but be sure to wait until after September 1st.

*We're in the midst of an energy shortage. Right? Well, a Florida man has figured out a way to help. He has designed and built a "gasifier" for his Lincoln Continental that will let him use wood as fuel. He is said to have learned the technology in Denmark during World War II. It doesn't sound bad to me, because he gets 3200 miles per cord.

*A government report released this summer showed that the National Forests drew more recreation use during 1980 than any other federal lands. There were 234.9 million visitor days recorded in the National Forests in 1980, amounting to 43 percent of the total. Army Corps of Engineers facilities drew 32 percent, and the National Parks drew 16 percent. National Forests continue to be very, very popular with all types of outdoor enthusiasts.

*Nationwide, the Forest Service employs many senior citizens, most of them part-time under the Senior Community Service Employment Program. Still others are working under full-time Forest Service appointments. "Pappy" Christianson, of the Klamath National Forest in California, is the oldest permanent Forest Service employee in the country. He is 80 years old and was only 4 at the time the Forest Service began in 1905. Pappy drives 200 miles a week in a pickup truck, doing maintenance work at eight campgrounds. He plans to keep working as long as he passes his annual physical examination. Pappy says he'll retire, "when I get old."

August 17, 1981 -

The increased emphasis on energy conservation, coupled with rapidly rising heating costs, has forced most Americans to make changes in their homes and/or their heating systems. Just a few short years ago it was uncommon for anyone to spend money improving the heating efficiency of their homes. Fuel oil, gas, electric, etc. were fairly cheap, so it didn't make good economic sense to spend several hundred dollars just to save a few dollars here and there on heating bills. And very few people were genuinely concerned about saving energy.

How quickly things change! The days of cheap heat and energy unawareness are gone forever. Now almost everyone is adding insulation to their attics and walls, lowering their thermostats, installing storm windows, and caulking or weather stripping around every crack and crevice.

Perhaps the most significant change that has occurred recently is the large number of homes that are being heated by wood. The increase in firewood demand has had quite an impact on National Forest management. We try to have enough free firewood (home use only) available to meet everyone's needs. However, it's becoming more and more difficult to do so. In 1973 we issued only about 25 or 30 firewood permits the entire Fall and Winter. This year we have already issued over 1000 permits between the Athens and Marietta Units of the Wayne National Forest. With this many people wanting firewood, it has been difficult to meet the demand.

Still, we realize the importance of the firewood program to the public. The Wayne National Forest is currently studying the problem and will be trying hard to come up with new ways to meet future demands for firewood.

Here are a few reminders for those people who have firewood permits:

1. Remember! The wood is for personal, home use only; it cannot be sold or traded for other goods.

2. There is a 5 cord limit. Don't get more than your share; leave some wood for others.

3. Stay within the designated area. The boundaries are clearly marked.

4. If you're cutting standing trees, make sure the stumps you leave are less than 12 inches high.

5. Failure to follow the regulations specified on the permit will result in losing your permit and paying a fine.

6. There's a lot of wood available, some easier to get to than others. The easy wood goes first, but with a little effort you should be able to get what you need.

In the future we hope we can come up with new ways to meet the ever increasing demand for firewood.

RANGER'S NOTEBOOK- We recently opened a firewood area on County Road 9 in the Pine Ridge area. It's in Independence Township between Deucher and Schley. The area is marked with a blue paint boundary all around, and there are 3 "Firewood Area" signs posted which are visible from County 9. All trees within the painted boundary may be cut, but not the boundary trees themselves. If you want a firewood permit, just stop by our office on Rt. 7 in Reno. We hope to get additional areas set up before Fall in other parts of Washington and Monroe Counties.

August 24, 1981 -

Friday, August 21 ended our 6-week Youth Conservation Corps (YCC) program. The 7 YCC'ers, all from Washington and Monroe Counties, worked very hard, accomplishing quite a variety tasks. In addition, approximately 25% of their time was spent in some aspect of environmental education. Each person said he/she (there were 4 boys and 3 girls) was very glad to have had the opportunity to work outdoors this summer in our program. It's always been that way. Since 1971 the best recruiting tool we've had for each year's YCC Camp has been the positive comments from the past campers.

This year's campers, aged 15-18, worked at a variety of jobs, including:

1) Construction of two, large portal signs along State Route 7. These signs, identifying the "Wayne National Forest," will serve as information signs to travelers for years to come. One sign was erected in Monroe County, near Fly, while the other one went up in Washington County, near Newport. These signs will complement the two existing ones on State Route 26 - one just south of Woodsfield and one just east of Marietta.

Below is a picture of one of the signs.

Back row (l-r) – Keith Hannahs, Pam Conley, Sheryl Jones, Rex Armstrong, Russ Fickiesen, Susie Rake.

Front row-(l-r) - Dave Greenwood, Mike Stevens, Todd Boney, John Kerr, Ed Payne.

2) The campers completed over 15 miles of trail maintenance on the Lamping Homestead Trail, the Ohio View Trail, and the River Trail. This consisted primarily of brushing, clipping, pruning, and removing large obstacles which had fallen across the trails.

3) The crew spent almost 2 weeks of their time working on the YCC buildings out near Bloomfield. They did a variety of projects there including, painting the

exterior of the water tank and coating the interior, staining the 6 buildings, repairing and erecting 2 gates, and light maintenance in the kitchen building.

4) Recreation maintenance and cleanup jobs at Leith Run Picnic Area, Lamping Homestead, and Hune Bridge, including painting bulletin boards and toilets, picking up litter, and brushing and clipping weeds.

5) Helping clean up, seed and mulch around the old home and building sites at Deucher on County Road 9.

6) And last, they spent their final work day here at our office helping to move most of our miscellaneous outside tools, supplies, outbuildings, etc., over to our new office location. This was a big help in making our August 28 move a smooth transition. (By the time you read this, we'll be in our new office, just 2 doors up from our old location.)

We appreciate the fine work Ed Payne accomplished with his YCC Crew. Ed always does a real good job directing our YCC program - coordinating the work projects with the environmental education. Ed and his crew certainly helped us through the busy summer season. We wish the entire crew-Keith Hannahs from Marietta, Pam Conley from Sardis, Sheryl Jones from Wingett Run, Rex Armstrong from Rinard Mills, Russ Fickiesen from Dart, Susie Rake from Whipple, and Mike Stevens from Marietta, success in their future endeavors. Todd Boney returned from the previous year to serve as this summer's Senior Camper and assist with supervisory and crew leader duties.

August 31, 1981 -

We've had quite a few people come in to the office lately and ask about camping on National Forest areas that are not developed campgrounds. Basically, camping is allowed on almost all sections of the Wayne National Forest. There are a few rules and guidelines that need to be followed however:

1)   Camping is allowed (without a fee) on all areas, unless otherwise posted. Exceptions would be developed campgrounds (a fee is required at those), boat launching areas, archaeological sites, picnic areas, or any other "special" areas;

2)   Any garbage, cans, bottles, or other litter must be taken when you leave;

3)   Dispose of human waste at least 100 feet from any water. Dig a small hole 6-8 inches deep and then cover it up. Natural bacterial decomposition will take place.

4)   Dispose of all waste water and wash water away from lakes, streams, and springs. Boil or treat all water before drinking it.

5)   Bring your own tent poles and stakes. Don't cut tree limbs and boughs to sleep on. It is illegal to

cut or dig any living vegetation. This includes small brush and shrubs, as well as trees.

6)   Firewood cannot be cut down. You can only use dead and down wood that you find laying around. Firewood is scarce in many areas. Therefore, for cooking we recommend taking a small, portable stove with you. If you have a campfire, keep it safe and small. Shelter it from wind, and keep it away from nearby logs, brush, and trees. Clear out a small circle to mineral soil in which to build your fire.   If available put a ring of rocks around it. When you're done, make sure the fire is dead out. Scatter the rocks and cover the black, burned circle with leaves and twigs. (Several of these black circles in a small area can be very unsightly).

7)   Plan your trip. Know the area and the predicted weather. Carry extra clothes, a map, first aid kit, compass, etc. Be sure that a friend or relative knows where you'll be, in case of emergencies.

Follow these few simple rules and you can enjoy a camping trip on almost any area of the Wayne National Forest.

RANGER'S NOTEBOOK - The first 4-year professional curriculum in Forestry was started at Cornell

University in Ithaca, New York in 1898. In the same year the Biltmore Forest School, a private school, was started in North Carolina. The Yale Forest School was established in 1900, offering a graduate curriculum in Forestry leading to a master's degree. During the next 5 years, Forestry programs were begun at the Universities of Michigan, Maine, Nebraska, Minnesota, the State Forest Academy in Pennsylvania, and Colorado College. Soon to follow were Harvard, Michigan State, and Iowa State as the Forestry profession began to grow in this country.

September 14, 1981 -

Now that the trees are starting to display their Fall wardrobes many people have asked, "What makes the leaves change colors?" In order to explain that, I first need to explain what makes leaves green.

A leaf is green because of the presence of a group of pigments known as chlorophylls. When they are abundant in the leaf's cells, as they are during the growing season, the chlorophylls' green dominates and masks out the colors of any other pigments that may be present in the leaf.

Chlorophyll's vital function is to capture the sun's energy and use it to produce the plant's food - simple sugars from water and carbon dioxide. In their food manufacturing process the chlorophylls are continually being used up. During the growing season they are replaced by the plant so that the supply remains high and the leaves stay green.

But as autumn approaches factors both inside and outside the plant cause the chlorophylls to be replaced more slowly than they are being used up. When this happens the green "masking" effect slowly fades away. Then other pigments that have been present all during the leaf's life begin to show through. These are called carotenoids. Their brilliant yellows and oranges tint the leaves of such hardwood species as hickories, ash, maple, yellow-poplar, black cherry and sassafras.

The reds, the purples, and their blended combinations that decorate the autumn foliage come from another group of pigments called anthocyanins. These pigments are not present in the leaf throughout the growing season like the carotenoids. Instead, they develop in later summer as the result of complex chemical interactions. The brighter the light during this period, the greater the production of anthocyanins and the more brilliant the resulting color display that we see. When the days of autumn are bright and cool, and the nights are chilly but not freezing, the brightest colorations usually develop.

In our autumn forests anthocyanins show up vividly in the maples, oaks, sourwood, sweetgum, dogwood and persimmon. These same pigments often combine with the carotenoids' colors to give us the deeper orange, fiery reds and bronzes typical of many hardwood species.

It may be a good thing to know that the leaves change colors because of complex chemical interactions that are influenced by many things such as the amount and intensity of light and the temperature. But it's kind of fun to daydream about Mother Nature walking through the forest dressing up her trees in new fall outfits. Naturally she would give the prettiest suits to her favorite trees.

Or maybe you picture Jack Frost as the one who does all the work. He sneaks in at night with buckets and buckets of paint and creates the splendid tapestry of colors that October is so famous for. But one thing is certain about the leaves changing colors ---- even the worst pessimist can't deny the beauty of it all. The Wayne National Forest offers thousands of acres in which you can enjoy this magnificent color display.

RANGER'S NOTEBOOK - Part of a poem by Will Carleton sums up most everyone's feelings about Fall:

"Sweet and smiling are thy ways,
Beauteous, golden Autumn days."

September 21, 1981 –

We're right in the middle of squirrel hunting season already. Time sure flies! Summer is gone and Fall is here - recent temperatures can attest to that.

The squirrel population in this area seems to be fairly high. Both of our local State Game Protectors - Jim Baker in Monroe County and Clifford Winstanley in Washington County - are expecting a good harvest of squirrels this year.

One thing though - the hickories didn't produce many nuts this year, at least not where I've looked. This being the case could account for the high number of squirrels I've seen crossing the roads lately. They could be migrating from last year's hickory areas to adjacent oak stands in search of food. Most of the oaks, and the walnuts, seem to have had good years.

In any case, both Game Protectors agree that the squirrels are out there. So put in your time hunting and you'll come home with a fine tasting meal. (It's hard to beat squirrel, gravy, biscuits, and mashed potatoes).

The last day of squirrel season on private lands is November 14, while on public lands (such as the Wayne National Forest) the last day to hunt is December 19.

Good luck to all of you!

*All good hunters will agree that the irresponsible hunter should not be tolerated. Any State Game

Protector can give you information about Hunter Training Courses. These are excellent courses that teach not only safety, but hunting ethics. Recently, cases of littering, trespassing and exceeding the bag limit have drawn attention. Good hunters must realize that the bad hunters can give the wrong image to all hunting. If you see any violations -- littering, destruction of property, or anything else -- report them to the State Game Protector for your County.

If possible, get the person's name and address, or maybe his vehicle make, model, and license number. Note the exact location of the violation. Jot down any other pertinent facts and contact the Game Protector as soon as possible.

Hunters are like any other group - most are ethical and responsible, but a few bad ones can spoil the bunch. I urge you to obey all Game Laws, and........ have a successful hunting season!

*Gifford Pinchot was one of the first professional Foresters in America. He was also the first Chief of the U.S. Forest Service. Here is one of the many quotes he made that still pertains to the management of our National Forests. "There are many great interests on the National Forests which sometimes conflict a little. They must all be made to fit into one another so that the machine runs smoothly as a whole. It is often necessary for one man to give way a little here, another a little there. But by giving way a little at present they both profit by it a great deal in the end.

"National Forests exist today because the people want them. To make them accomplish the most good the people themselves must make clear how they want them to run."

September 28, 1981 -

A fisherman friend of mine stopped by the other day and pretty soon we were talking about "the one that got away." Then we started swapping Air Force stories, talking about poisonous snakes, and stalking wild, dangerous animals. (All of this done while surrounded by the safety of the chain link fence in my backyard).

Anyway, he mentioned a tale his granddad told about encountering a mountain lion over in West Virginia about the year 1900, and how it was a shame there weren't any mountain lions in the eastern United States any longer.

I said, "Hold on just a minute! There are a lot of people, myself included, who think that the big cat just might still roam portions of our eastern mountains."

A long discussion followed. It reminded me of an article I wrote two years ago for a newspaper in north

Georgia. Some people agree with me, others disagree. But I believe there just may be mountain lions in the East. In any case, it provides for interesting discussions (especially when surrounded by a chain link fence in your own backyard)!

I hope you enjoy the following:

The Eastern Panther, or mountain lion, is thought by most people to be a thing of the past. Many even believe the animal is extinct. But evidence gathered in the last few years is so strong that it is very likely the big cat actually survived in the East and is, in fact, growing in numbers.

Some local oldtimers still living can probably remember seeing panthers in the mountains. At one time they were fairly common. But in the last 50 or 60 years the panther seemed to have disappeared, and the occasional sightings were passed off as either someone's wild imagination or possibly a large bobcat.

Other names that mountain folks gave the panther, or mountain lion, were catamount (for cat of the mountains), big cat, and "painter" (a slang for panther). Throughout the Appalachian Mountains today, names like Big Cat Mountain, Painter Knob, Panther Creek, and Painter Run are quite common and point out that the big animal was once widespread in the East.

The strongest evidence to date of the Eastern panther's existence comes from West Virginia. In that state the last reported killing of a panther had been in 1908. And although some people claimed the big cat still roamed the high mountains, there was never any real proof - that is, until 1976. In April of that year a farmer shot and killed a panther that was attacking his sheep in Pocahontas County, near the Monongahela National Forest. One week later, a pregnant panther was captured in the same county; it now resides at the French Creek Game Farm near Buckhannon, West Virginia. Though many people questioned where the animals actually came from, scientists who studied the two cats confirmed that they were, indeed, Eastern mountain lions.

And like they say, "a panther in the hand is worth two in the bush". Or something like that. Proof positive now existed that the big cat still survived.

Are there panthers in the mountains of North Georgia? It's quite possible that there are. There have been reports of sightings in Union, Towns, and Rabun Counties. And these sightings are becoming more common throughout the Eastern mountains - all the way from Canada to Georgia. Sightings have been made in Maine, New Hampshire, New York, Pennsylvania, Virginia, West Virginia, North Carolina, and other states. A hiker in New York's Adirondack Mountains took a picture (which seems to be authentic) of a panther he saw in the mountains. Closer home, sightings in the Great Smokey Mountains and near the Blue Ridge

Parkway are being made frequently. A trails foreman in the Great Smokey Mountain National Park even sighted a panther chasing a wild boar on the Appalachian Trail. So you can bet that there are a few panthers in North Georgia, too.

I think the animal still survives. And I'm glad. I'd hate to see the panther go the way of the passenger pigeon and other extinct animals.

If anyone sights a panther it can be reported at our office. And better yet, if tracks are seen, particularly in the snow, we will report this to a researcher who is stationed at Clemson University, over in South Carolina.

Whether or not you believe the big cat still roams the mountains, one thing is certain. There's enough believable evidence on hand to make you wonder.

<u>RANGER'S NOTEBOOK-</u>

The Eastern mountain lion is protected under the Endangered Species Act of 1973, which makes it illegal to hunt or kill the animal.

October 12, 1981 -

WOOD BURNING FACTS AND HINTS

A fireplace adds a certain charm to a room or den. It is also adequate for getting rid of early morning and evening chills in the Spring or Fall (not in Winter). A fireplace can also be a real lifesaver if your electricity is off for several days during a winter ice storm. But, all things considered, a fireplace is not an effective or efficient means of heating your home (or even a single room). During the cold winter months, not even the most elaborate fireplaces (complete with all gadgets, etc.) will help you heat your home. In fact, you'll very likely have a net loss in heat output. The primary reason for this is that a fireplace draws large quantities of warm air from your home and this warm air is lost out the chimney. It is replaced by cool outside air. For heat efficiency, modern wood burning stoves are best since they have draft controls that draw much smaller quantities of air than a fireplace. These metal stoves also retain heat for long periods of time and this heat radiates into your home.

Last year more than 7.3 million green tons of free firewood were picked up on National Forest land. This compared to only 1.1 million in 1973.

Federal experts estimate that there is a minimum of 500 million dry tons of residue wood in public forests, private woodlands, and city clearing sites that could be turned into wood heat.

Wood now makes up about 2% of our nation's fuel supply. Experts figure this could easily be increased to 7%, which would save more than 2.5 million barrels of oil a day.

Firewood should be dried a minimum of 3 months before burning and preferably 6 months. The drier your wood the more heat it gives off and the less creosote build-up you get. Many people prefer using a lot of green wood because it lasts longer in the stove than dry wood. However, it is false that because it lasts longer that it gives off more heat. Here's why. Green wood contains a high percentage of water, resins, and oils. It takes much of the heat from your fire just to evaporate this moisture from the wood for it to burn, thus resulting in a cooler fire. And cooler fires always mean a quicker creosote buildup in your chimney.

Your chimney should be cleaned at least a couple of times a year to prevent creosote buildup. If constructing a new chimney, make sure it rises high enough above the roof line to get a good draw and prevent downdrafts. Downdrafts can also cause more than normal creosote formation. A new chimney cap, open on 4 sides with the top closed, will help prevent downdrafts.

<u>**October 19, 1981 -**</u>

MORE WOOD BURNING HINTS AND FACTS

The fuel value of wood varies, depending upon species, density, and moisture content. While any wood will burn, the denser hardwoods make the best fuel because they burn slower and give off more heat per unit of volume than the lighter woods.

Actually, a ton of air-dry wood of any species contains about the same amount of heat potential. The problem is that because of differences in density, it takes much more wood of certain species to make a ton than others. For instance, think how many more sticks of yellow-poplar it would take to weigh a ton than it would white oak or hickory. But a ton of either species, dried to the same level, should provide about the same amount of heat.

Air drying wood for about 6 months will reduce its moisture content to approximately 20%. This is as dry as you can get most woods without going to artificial means, such as oven drying or kiln drying.

5,000 pounds of freshly cut white oak will weigh only 4,000 pounds when air dry. This means 1,000 pounds of moisture is gone from the wood that won't have to be evaporated off by your stove during burning, if only you'll let your wood dry for about 6 months. I know this isn't always possible, but it's sure worth it if you can.

Remember: burning green wood means: 1) a cooler fire, and 2) more creosote buildup in your chimney.

An air dry cord of white pine weighs only about half as much as an air dry cord of oak or hickory.

In the early 1800's in the Appalachian Mountains, it often took up to 20 or 25 cords of wood per year to heat a home using the fireplace. And even then, much of the house was very cool. Today's modern mountain homes, with insulation, better construction, and more efficient wood stoves, can be heated using only about 4 to 6 cords in the same size house. Some parts of the "good old days" weren't so good after all.

Here's an old poem about firewood that you see every so often:

Beech wood fires are bright and clear,
If the logs are kept a year.
Chestnut's only good, they say,
If for long it's laid away.
Birch and pine logs burn too fast,
Blaze up bright and do not last.
Elm wood burns like churchyard mold,
E'en the very flames are cold.
Poplar gives a bitter smoke,

Fills your eyes and makes you choke.

Apple wood will scent your room,

With an incense-like perfume.

Oak and maple, if dry and old,

Keep away the winter cold.

But ash wood wet or ash wood dry,

For a Queen to warm her slippers by.

__October 26, 1981 –__

Remembering from last week's article that the denser the wood the greater the heat output, here are relative heat values for some of our most common woods:

White Ash	-	High
Hickory	-	Very High
Sugar Maple	-	High
Red Maple	-	Medium
Gum	-	Medium
Mixed Oaks	-	High
Yellow Poplar	-	Low
Aspen	-	Low
White Pine	-	Low
Shortleaf Pine	-	Medium
Dogwood	-	Very High
Sassafras	-	Low

Different wood types leave different amounts of ash after burned. The ash residue of most woods will vary from 0.1 to 3.0 percent. Ash content can vary according to age, the part of the tree the wood comes from, and how much bark is included.

Either steel plate or cast iron are good materials for wood stoves, though both materials have positive and negative aspects. Both materials are good for heat retention. Steel can warp, but this won't normally affect the functioning of the stove. Cast iron can crack, but this doesn't often happen. Both materials can rust or eventually burn out. In general, the thicker the material, the longer it will last.

You can ruin your stove, stovepipe, and chimney by burning very much trash, especially plastics. Many plastics contain chlorine and fluorine, which form very corrosive acids in a fire. Stovepipe can corrode clear through in just a year under such conditions.

Though steel can warp, cast iron can crack, and either one can corrode, using firebrick or other liners will lessen these affects. This lining will keep the main stove body from getting too hot, and the linings are easily replaced.

It's a good idea for everyone to have a smoke alarm or two in their home. The newer models are very dependable and can last for a year on just one battery. A wood-caused fire will give off smoke that can easily be detected by a smoke alarm, thus setting off the buzzer. These devices have saved thousands of lives in the past several years.

November 2, 1981 –

Have you ever heard of the Bee Bee tree? Probably not! Until about two months ago, I hadn't either. But, Mr. Arnold Davis of Longacres, in Reno, has heard of the tree. In fact, he has a couple of them growing in his yard. The two trees have been there for over 20 years. Here's how I "discovered" the Bee Bee tree.

Last summer our preacher at Reno Christian Church, Howard McGinnis, told me he knew a Mr. Davis in Reno who had a couple of unusual trees growing in his yard. (Howard is a real outdoorsman, and we're always talking about trees or hunting or fishing or something - but that's another story). Anyway, Howard and I decided we'd visit Mr. Davis and talk to him about his trees. Well, it kind of fell by the wayside until September when my oldest son, Jeff, was making a leaf collection for his 7th grade science class. We thought the Bee Bee leaf would make an interesting addition to his collection. Howard and I went to see the tree, Jeff got an unusual leaf for his book, and we had the chance to talk to a most interesting person - Mr. Arnold Davis.

Mr. Davis and his wife obtained the seeds for the Bee Bee tree in 1957 from the Morris Arboretum, which is at the University of Pennsylvania. They had always been interested in plants and gardening, and they have enough of a variety of trees in the yard to make any amateur botanist proud. (In addition to the Bee Bee tree and lots of flowers and shrubs, you will find the following trees - holly, persimmon, mimosa, blue spruce, Norway spruce, linden (basswood), sugar & red maples, mountain-ash, sweetgum, and others).

The Bee Bee tree, scientific name <u>Evodia daniellii,</u> first became popular in this country back in the early to mid-fifties. It was recognized as being potentially important to bee keepers because the tree blooms at a time when other nectar-yielding blossoms are scarce (from late July well into August). I missed seeing it in bloom this year, but Mr. Davis says that the beautiful white blooms nearly cover up the entire tree. The tree will grow to about forty feet high, and has been planted in some areas for shade and ornamental purposes. They say that honeybees like the trees and actively work them when they are found.

It was very interesting talking with Mr. Davis and learning about the Bee Bee tree. (Oh yes, he said that he was originally told that the tree was native to Africa, but more recently was told that it came from Korea, so he's not sure. Perhaps some of our beekeeper friends can tell us).

RANGER'S NOTEBOOK

How many different species of trees do you think can be found locally? Jeff and I drove around town one Sunday afternoon, and the numbers amazed us. He had 112 different leaves in his collection: And I'm sure we missed a lot more. He had everything from American Chestnut and Chinese Chestnut, to Cypress, Dawn Redwood, Cucumbertree, Balsam Fir, Paw Paw, Honey Locust, Osage-orange, and several kinds of Hickories, Maples, and Oaks. Of the 112 leaves he collected, I estimate that around 70 to 75 are native to the local area. Living in the foothills of the Appalachian Mountains as we do here, we are surrounded by as wide a diversity of trees as can probably be found anywhere in the United States.

November 9, 1981 –

Fall is nearly half over now. The last week or so seems to have been signaling the start of Winter and the end of Fall. The change is usually gradual and doesn't catch us totally by surprise, though.

Most of us would agree that we're very lucky to be living where we can enjoy the distinct beauty of each of the four seasons. California, Arizona, and Florida are all nice places, but without the true change of seasons something just doesn't seem right. I spent a year living in Arizona while in the Air Force, and it was indeed a beautiful place with lots of interesting sights to see; but I sure did miss the Fall and Winter.

In the mid to southern Appalachians, our Winters aren't normally so severe that we can't enjoy them. The Winters here are nothing like those in Minnesota or Maine; and in Minnesota you have such a short Summer and Fall that they're gone before you realize it. Here in southeastern Ohio our four seasons are just about equally balanced.

The Appalachian Mountain area is also perhaps the most beautiful section of our country in terms of diversity of plant life and physical features. The Rocky Mountains have their awesome and majestic splendor, but they sure don't have the colorful beauty of Fall like the Appalachians do. And some of the mid-western states that are colorful in the Fall, certainly don't have the mountains and other physical features that we have in the Appalachians. Here we've got the best of both.

A couple of weeks ago, I took a drive along State Route 800 between Woodsfield and Fly. At the time the colors were beautiful. I don't think you could have found a more scenic route to travel at that time. As we drove down along Trail Run and then past where Ludolph Ridge comes into Route 800, the sights were splendid. The view from the hill overlooking Fly toward the Ohio River and beyond -- you'd have to travel many miles to find a better one.

Driving back toward Reno on Route 7, we turned up County Road 14 at Wade, where Reas Run comes into the Ohio River. About 3 miles north, the road junctions with County 9 (at Deucher), and we turned to head west out Pine Ridge. Here's another very scenic route to drive, especially in the Fall. (You can pick up Washington County Road 9 in Reno and follow it northeast until it runs into State Route 260 at Yellow House, about 2 miles west of New Matamoras. Total distance one way is about 20 miles). As we drove on out Pine Ridge toward Schley the view was great! There are a couple of places where you can look out to the south-east over the rolling ridges toward the Ohio River and beyond into West Virginia. It ranks with scenic views anywhere. At Schley we turned on to County Road 25 and followed it south into Newport.

There are many things to be thankful for as we approach the Holiday Season, not the least of which is the beauty of the area where we live.

November 16, 1981 –

The 154 National Forests in this country are managed under the principles of multiple-use and sustained yield. Multiple-use means that a variety of activities can occur, such as recreation, timber management, wildlife management, etc. Sustained yield means that these resources are managed so as to produce outputs indefinitely. When speaking of the timber resource, it becomes evident that to manage for a sustained yield the older timber must be cut and utilized, and that there must always be a wide-ranging mix of younger trees growing. This across-the-board variety of age classes results in a healthy plant diversity and a needed mixture of different wildlife habitats.

The National Forests of the United States currently have timber stands with an estimated volume of 1,055 billion board feet. This ranges from the Sitka spruce of Alaska and the Douglas-fir of the West, to the fast-growing pines of the South and the high-quality hardwoods of the Appalachian Mountain forests.

The sale of National Forest timber has averaged about 12.5billion board feet per year since 1960. This has amounted to nearly 30 percent of all sawtimber cut in this country. Most of this harvest is concentrated in the West. However, quite a bit of timber is cut in the East, also. About 4 million board feet per year is sold between the Athens and Marietta Units of the Wayne National Forest.

The Forest Service itself does not cut timber, but rather sells it to commercial operators or local residents who depend upon it for their livelihoods. The volume of timber sold is determined by a Management Plan, which is prepared by professional foresters. This Plan takes into account many factors, such as age, location, species, health condition, impacts on other resources, etc.

The size of a timber sale may be small, such as 5-10 acres totaling only several thousand board feet or it may be many acres in size for over a million board feet. The larger timber sales are advertised for bid, usually for 30 days, while smaller sales can be offered without advertising. The prospective bidders have a chance to look at the timber on the ground and make their own estimates before making their bid. If a bidder is successful, a contract is signed, a performance bond is posted, and the cutting begins. Forest Service contracts provide for a pay-as- you-cut operation, with payment being made in advance of cutting.

Twenty-five percent of the receipts from selling timber and from other sources is returned to the counties in which the National Forests are located. This money is then used for schools and roads in those areas. If you're interested in future timber sales in this area, call our office for more information or to get your name on the bidders list – 373-9055.

<u>RANGER'S NOTEBOOK</u> –

With the recent interest in commercial firewood operations we have several smaller areas that can be sold on a first-come, first-serve basis. One 8 acre tract in southern Monroe County can be sold for less than $600.00 and has many, many good cords of firewood available on it. And there are others, too. If you'd be interested in a firewood sale, don't hesitate to contact us.

<u>November 23, 1981</u> -

How time flies! It seems like just yesterday it was summertime. But the kids have been in school almost 3 months now, we just had our first snowfall, and Sunday night it was down to 18 degrees. So I know it's not summer any longer! So much for wishful thinking.

Anyway, we've got the Holiday Season coming up, and plenty to be thankful <u>for</u>. (Please, English teachers, don't get mad because I ended the last sentence with a preposition. I do it all the time. See RANGER'S NOTEBOOK at the end of this column).

Snuggled right in between Thanksgiving and Christmas comes a time that many people look forward to (whoops, I did it again). It's deer hunting season. In Ohio the season runs from Monday, November 30 thru Saturday, December 5. You West Virginia readers have an extra week over there --- from November 23 thru December 5. From all indications, the deer population is high and hunters should enjoy a successful season; maybe even set some harvest records if the weather stays right.

Wayne National Forest Wildlife Biologist, Dennis Krusac, told me that the deer seem to be in full rut now (in other words, mating season is close to its peak). He's noticed plenty of scrapes in the woods the past few days. In this part of the country the rut lasts a couple of months, with the peak generally occurring sometime in November.

This fact seems to be proven also, by the road kill figures for deer. Dispatcher Beth McCutcheon, of the State Highway Patrol office in Reno, said the number of deer-caused automobile accidents is always highest in November. During mating season deer movement picks up dramatically, so you'll normally see more of them during this time. Also, the bucks in particular, have other things on their minds than being careful crossing roads.

Thus, the scene is set for some bad accidents. Slow down a little, and be extra careful driving this month. Highway Patrol figures for the last 5 years show the following <u>reported</u>, deer-related accidents locally:

	Oct.	Nov.	yearly total
1977 –	- 30	39	207
1978 –	- 21	62	202
1979 –	-15	52	202
1980 –	- 21	59	212
1981 –	- 24	41	175

(thru 11/22/81)

Statewide, about 40% of the total number of accidents occurs during October and November.

Mike Budzik, Private Lands Wildlife Biologist for the Ohio Department of Natural Resources, has high expectations for this season.

"Statewide we're expecting upwards of 230,000 hunters this year, which would be a record number," he said. "Also, there are more counties open to deer hunting now than previously. These two factors, coupled with our high deer herd levels, could mean a record harvest."

Mike said the 20-county southeastern Ohio area probably gets the most hunting pressure. This, of course, includes all of the Wayne National Forest. He also told me that the deer population may be a little too high in some areas, as indicated by the increasing number of complaints from landowners about crop damage. The harvest figures he gave me for 1980 were Monroe County - 791 and Washington County - 1579.

State Game Protectors Jim Baker for Monroe County and Cliff Winstanley for Washington County are gearing up for their busiest time of the year.

Cliff told me, "The eastern part of Washington County seems to have more deer. It's a little more rugged than the rest of the county, too, which makes it more difficult to hunt. I would say the areas in the Wayne National Forest would be excellent hunting."

Cliff is predicting record harvests this year if the weather is right. ("Just enough snow for good tracking," he said). The deer herd estimate for this county is 8 to 9 per square mile, which, if my arithmetic is right, means over 5,000 deer county-wide.

The Monroe County population is up, too, according to Baker. "Road kills have been frequent. The population here is probably 6 or more per square mile", Jim said. He listed Perry, Washington, and Benton Townships as probably the best hunting.

West Virginia DNR Biologist, Jim Hill, is located just across the river in Parkersburg, and he handles the counties that adjoin the Ohio River, including Wood, Pleasants, Tyler and Wetzel. "Our herd levels are very high right now," he told me, "maybe even as high as 15-20 per square mile. We get a lot of out-of-state hunters, and about 4 out of 5 of those are from Ohio." He's predicting a harvest to exceed the record set in 1979.

Winstanley and Baker were unanimous in listing 3 items to stress to hunters:

1)   Wear blaze orange! Deer are color blind anyway. With the number of hunters in the woods, don't take any chances.

2)   Don't trespass! Be sure to obtain a landowner's permission before hunting on private property.

3)   Hunting hours are 7:00 a.m. to 5:00 p.m. If you're in the woods outside these times, you cannot have your gun loaded.

(Jim Baker has a new phone number, so if you're in Monroe County and need to get in touch with him, he said to call 472-5773).

Checking stations for this year are: **Washington County** --- Lane's Sporting Goods in Marietta, Alma's Coffee Shop in New Matamoras, Fisher's Sportabout in

Waterford, Bishop's Sporting Goods in Lowell, and Vincent Gun Shop in Vincent.

Monroe County --- Carson's Carryout in Wilson, Able's cheese House in Sardis, Dotta's Pennzoil in Clarington, Highman's Grocery in Graysville, and the Monroe Wildlife Area. And remember, this year if you kill a deer you must check it in personally. No one else can do it for you.

Good luck, and have a safe, successful deer season!

RANGER'S NOTEBOOK - Sir Winston Churchill didn't like the grammar rule that says --- 'Don't end a sentence with a preposition'. "Balderdash," he is said to have exclaimed: "That is nonsense up with which we shouldn't have to put." I think I agree with Sir Winston. He convinced me with that one sentence (up with which I'm glad I don't have to put; or, I mean, which I don't have to put up <u>with</u>).

November 30, 1981 -

The old Ring House in Benton Township, Monroe County is one of the most interesting places in this area. It's located at Poulton, just west of Jericho, right beside the Little Muskingum River. At one time in addition to the house, there was also a barn, chicken house, other dwellings nearby, and, of course, the sawmill and grain mill on the river bank just below a dam. The area, naturally, became known as Ring's Mill.

A couple of weeks ago I met Clifford and Earl Ring at the old house. The piece of land that the old house stands on is now part of the Wayne National Forest. The Rings are interested in doing what they can to preserve or protect the old house. So is the Forest Service. Even though we now have a restricted budget, and money is tight, we're going to work together and see what can be done in the next couple of years.

We have plans to develop a canoe access point at Ring's Mill, with accompanying parking lot, turn-around area, and possibly a few picnic tables. It will be similar to our canoe access at Hune Bridge in Washington County. Depending on our budget we hope to do this later this fiscal year or the next. We'd like to do some interpretive signing to explain a little about the history of the site.

The house that is still standing is referred to as the Ring House, or the Old Stone House. A couple of years ago it was nominated and accepted for inclusion on the National Register, as one of the few houses of its type left standing in Ohio.

Clifford Ring sent me some notes on his family's history, which included the following:

"The Ring name seems to be of English origin, with the Rings coming to this country in the 1700's and settling in New York. Around 1812 the Ring's moved into the Ohio frontier and settled in Belmont County. The men of the Ring family were millers, and wherever they went they continued this profession. Then in about 1835, Walter Ring and two sons came to Monroe County, along the Little Muskingum River, to start a new mill. They built a log house, returned to Belmont County, and then brought the rest of the family back to Monroe County to live the following Spring. Land was cleared, and a farm started.

In 1840 work began on the stone house that still stands today. It was completed in 1846. (Clifford said that the stones used to build the house were quarried on the hills above the river. As we stood talking, we both agreed what a great task it must have been to haul the huge stones off the hill, across the river, and then build a 2-story house out of them). The mill itself wasn't completed until 1848 but what a structure it was! It stood 5 stories high and was 28 feet square. The millstones were brought down from Pennsylvania and weighed 1600 pounds. Now they were back into milling full time, along with keeping the farm going, and by 1850 had begun another related occupation. They built a sawmill, beside the grain mill, which sawed lumber that found its way to many places, including Cincinnati. The water to power the 2 mills came from a 7-foot high dam which was constructed of logs and rock boulders.

Throughout the rest of the 1800's the Ring family was to be one of the prominent families of Monroe County. Around 1882 a covered bridge was built over the Little Muskingum. Until that time, depending upon the season of the year, anyone coming from the other side of the river had to ford it or come over on a john boat. And of course the boys found a special challenge in walking across the mill dam.

The bridge stood until it was replaced by a steel structure in 1955. The mill itself operated until 1921 when a hard winter ice flow washed out the dam. The mill was torn down a few years later. As far as the stone house goes, someone lived in it as recently as the mid-1960's, and it's still in remarkably good shape."

Perhaps if all goes well, we can re-roof the structure and preserve this amazing building, which serves as a monument and memorial both to the early settlers in general, and the Ring family in particular.

December 7, 1981 –

<u>BITS & PIECES</u>
*President Reagan recently signed into law new legislation doubling fines and increasing other penalties

for violating the Lacey Act. This Act is the nation's oldest and most basic wildlife protection law. The Lacey Act makes it illegal to transport in interstate or foreign commerce any wildlife that is taken, possessed, bought, or sold in violation of the laws of States or other countries. Originally passed in 1900, the law now has sufficient penalties to discourage the illegal trade in increasingly high-profit wildlife products (crocodile handbags sell in Europe for $400 to $1200 dollars apiece and there is a purple parrot that brings $8,000 in the United States). The illegal trade is a detriment to the honest dealers, who import and export over a half-billion dollars of goods each year.

*It's a sign of the times. With increasing costs of heating with electric and fossil fuels, many people have turned to wood heat. Vermont recently became the first state where wood is the primary source of home heat. About 41% of Vermont's homes are heated by wood. Fuel oil came in second place.

*Having been in Columbus again recently, I wonder why they don't call it the "Windy City." Have you ever been there when the wind wasn't blowing? Actually, the windiest city in the United States is Great Falls, Montana, where the average wind speed is 13.1 miles per hour. (That's out in the area of the Lewis and Clark

National Forest). I'm not sure where Columbus ranks, but Chicago, THE "Windy City", ranks only in 16th place.

*Here's a quote made by the first Chief of the U.S. Forest Service, Gifford Pinchot, in 1907. It's still very true today. "There are many great interests on the National Forests which sometimes conflict a little. They must all be made to fit into one another so that the machine runs smoothly as a whole. It is often necessary for one man to give way a little here, another a little there. But by giving way a little at present they both profit by it a great deal in the end."

*It seems like we're always hearing talk about billions of dollars these days. How much is a billion dollars? If you spent $1,000 a day, it would take you almost 3,000 years to spend it all!

*An outdoorsman friend of mine might have the right idea. He told me, "Since everyone should believe in something, I <u>believe</u> I'll go fishing." Sounds good to me! Well, I <u>believe</u> I'll end this column. So long till next week. Hope you all enjoy your - - - - Wayne National Forest.

December 14, 1981 -

I've had some people ask about the Christmas tree that is put up every December at our nation's Capitol in Washington, D.C. Where does the tree come from? What kinds of trees are used? When did the program begin? How does the U.S. Forest Service help select the tree?

The Capitol Christmas Tree program began in 1965, with the big push coming from Speaker of the House at that time, John McCormack. That year a live Douglas fir tree was selected and actually planted on the Capitol grounds. The thinking was to maintain a living symbol of the Christmas spirit and to re-use the tree in ceremonies each year. Unfortunately, after the 1968 season the tree died.

In 1969 the Forest Service became the agency responsible for the Capitol Christmas Tree program. That year 3 different trees were pieced together to make the one large tree. The results were not satisfactory. The tree was very difficult to put together and it didn't look that good either.

In 1970 the procedure for selecting the tree was again changed, and this procedure has remained in effect since that time. Basically, here's the process:

1) The tree is selected from forests east of the Mississippi River. (This involves Regions 8 and 9 of the U.S. Forest Service). The reason for this is that it would be very difficult to

transport a large tree from the Western United States all the way to the Capitol.

2)   Foresters working at the field level are asked to nominate potential trees, based on form, size, shape, and ease of removing it from the woods;

3)   The Architect from the U.S. Capitol, in conjunction with Forest Service officials, makes a final selection and on-the-ground inspection of the tree;

4)   The tree is carefully cut, removed from the woods, and transported in one piece to Washington, D.C.

Some local communities have even held going-away ceremonies for "their" tree and the townspeople then accompanied it by car caravan to the Capitol.

In 1970 the first tree was selected from the Monongahela National Forest in West Virginia; in 1971 it came from the Cherokee National Forest in Tennessee; and in 1972 it came from the White Mountain National Forest in New Hampshire. (I wasn't able to find what species of trees were used during those years). From 1973-80 the trees and their sources were:

1973 – White spruce	– Allegheny NF	– PA
1974 – Fraser fir	– Pisgah NF	– NC
1975 – Balsam fir	– Ottawa NF	– MI
1976 – Red spruce	– Monongahela NF	– WV

1977 – White spruce   – Nemadji SF   – MN

1978 – Norway spruce – Savage River SF   – MD

1979 – White spruce   – Nicolet NF   – WI

1980 – White spruce   – Green Mountain NF - VT

(NF – National Forest; SF – State Forest).

1981's tree is 65 years old and 52 feet tall. The white spruce, from Michigan's Hiawatha National Forest, will be lighted about 2 weeks before Christmas during a ceremony with several dignitaries attending and the Marine Corps band playing Christmas music. The tree is usually taken down on January 2.

The U.S. Forest Service is very proud to help coordinate the Capitol Christmas Tree program. Perhaps someday the Wayne National Forest will furnish the Nation's Christmas Tree.

December 21, 1981 –

After the last few days, I'm sure everyone has their cold weather clothing out; I know I sure do. My old coat is my most important piece of winter clothing. It's a goose down coat that I bought on sale a few years ago when prices weren't so high. It keeps me very warm. My two sons, Jeff and Brent, have vests and coats that they wear which contain the new synthetic fiber-fill material.

The boys seem to stay warm, for they never complain about being cold.

This brings up some interesting questions on the relative pros and cons of natural down versus the man-made materials.

Natural goose down is probably the most efficient insulating material available for clothing on a pound-for-pound basis. It is very lightweight and easily regains its fluffiness after normal compression. Down also "breathes", and thus body moisture will evaporate quite rapidly, eliminating any dampness problems.

One hint on selecting down clothing is that high quality items are made using prime northern goose down. You can get either duck or goose down, but most experts agree that goose down is the better of the two.

On the negative side, down will lose most of its insulating value when it gets wet. It also clumps up and doesn't dry out very fast. The synthetic fiber-fills, however, will still keep much of their insulating value even when wet. They also dry out quicker than down items.

For a weight comparison, down sleeping bags might weigh between 2 and $2^1/_2$ pounds, while the synthetic bags might weigh 4 pounds or more.

As far as cost goes, the synthetic fills are the best buys. For example, a very good goose down coat might cost $70 to $100, while a comparable fiber-fill coat might cost only $45 to $60.

Neither type of insulation can take extremely rough treatment. They both need to be handled carefully - don't wad them up or sit on them; store them by hanging them up; keep them away from moisture; don't store near heat; and make sure you have them cleaned according to instructions on the label.

In summary, if you want more durability and better tolerance to wet weather at a cheaper price, choose the synthetic material. If you want the most warmth and the least weight, then choose goose down. Either way, select your items carefully and enjoy the winter weather.

RANGER'S NOTEBOOK- All of us at the Wayne National Forest wish you and yours a very Merry Christmas and a Happy New Year.

December 28, 1981 –

Well, we sure hope everyone had a nice Christmas and that you're looking forward to a happy New Year. It's hard to believe it's 1982 already! Time sure flies.

We're looking forward to a busy year in 1982. We've had to cut back in a few areas because of budget reductions, but we still have a lot to do here on the Athens Ranger District. (As you know the Athens Ranger District includes two units

- the Marietta Unit and the Athens Unit). Some of the projects we have planned are:

Timber Sales - We'll be marking and selling over 3 million board feet of timber. The sales will be primarily on the Athens side, but we'd like to sell some timber on the Marietta Unit also. If you're interested, or know anyone who might be, give us a call.

Firewood - We hope to be able to meet the ever-increasing demand for home fuel wood by having several areas designated for free firewood. The areas will be set up this summer, and if you're interested, I suggest you stop by to get a permit early. The demand could well exceed our available supply. Also, we have a few small areas that can be sold to commercial firewooders at very reasonable prices. Wood taken from our free-use areas cannot be sold or traded; it must be for personal use only.

Site preparation - Many of our employees spend a portion of the year operating chainsaws and other equipment in old timber sale areas. They cut down many of the stunted and deformed trees, which allows the new, young tree seedlings to get the full sunlight they need in order to grow well.

Reforestation - Each year we plant tree seedlings in areas that are open or where tree growth has not been successful in the past. In designating these areas, special consideration is given to wildlife and other needs.

Wildlife management - This involves a variety of fish and wildlife habitat improvement work, such as establishing new wildlife openings, planting trees and shrubs for food, maintaining existing brushy areas, etc. This work is coordinated with the Ohio DNR - Division of Wildlife.

Reclamation of old stripmine areas - The Athens Unit recently completed reclamation of an old, abandoned stripmine area. More work is planned for this coming year. The areas are graded, seeded, topsoil brought in if needed, and are generally put back into a productive state. Erosion control and water quality improvement measures are also taken to help heal these old scars.

Recreation - Here on the Marietta Unit we have a boat launch and picnic area on the Ohio River at Leith Run (near Frontier High School); a picnic area, hiking trail, and small fishing lake at Lamping Homestead in Monroe County (just east of Marr on Rt. 537); a canoe access site at Hune Bridge on the Little Muskingum River (between Dart and Wingett Run); and over 15 miles of hiking trails. The Athens Unit has picnic areas, a campground, hiking trails, and a recently completed horseback riding trail.

Mineral activities - Much of our workload the past couple of years has been related to the increased oil & gas activity in southeastern Ohio. We expect this to continue during 1982. We anticipate approximately 100 new wells to be drilled on the Marietta Unit alone. Since most of the minerals under the Wayne National Forest are privately owned, our job is to try to coordinate drilling activity with our other resources. We help in access road layout, selecting well site locations, laying out pipeline systems, and inspecting these areas for proper reclamation. We work very closely with the Ohio DNR - Division of Oil & Gas, especially on reclamation items. As with many other groups, we've been overworked and undermanned in this area of minerals management. This year, however, we expect to be staffed a little better in Oil & Gas work, and this fact, along with the increasing cooperation and more systematic development by the oil & gas companies, will allow us to be more responsive as the situation develops.

These are not all the jobs we have to do. There are others, such as fighting forest fires, water sampling, road maintenance, land line location, cultural resource surveys, school talks and fairs, and more. All in all we have a busy year ahead and we're looking forward to it anxiously. We wish everyone a Happy New Year in 1982 from all of us here at your....WAYNE NATIONAL FOREST.

January 4, 1982 -

Winter hunting, camping, and hiking are enjoyable activities for many people; but they can also be very dangerous, or even fatal, if necessary preparations are not made or proper precautions are not taken. In the summertime minor errors in judgment usually result in only slight inconveniences. However, in the wintertime these same mistakes accumulate and multiply rapidly, with sometimes tragic results. The following thoughts should be useful to the winter outdoorsman:

1. Travel with a group, or at least with a partner. Then, in case of sickness or injury someone can go for help.

2. Lay out a reasonable travel route. Generally speaking, most people think they can walk much farther than they actually can. With winter days being very short and snow accumulation slowing your rate of speed, don't overestimate the distance that you plan to travel. If you're camping, be sure to set up camp early and not get caught by darkness.

3. Know your route well. Be aware of possible hazards. In this part of the country it is best to stay off of lakes or ponds even if the ice appears to be thick enough to walk on. A plunge in icy water, away from help, can be fatal.

4. Be prepared for the worst. Besides the cold temperatures, the winds are often very strong, particularly on mountains or ridge tops. Extreme wind chill factors can worsen the consequences of any problems you might encounter. At 10 degrees (F) above zero a 25 mile per hour

wind causes the chill factor to be 30 degrees below zero! In this instance exposed flesh can freeze within a very few minutes.

5. Be sure to let someone know where you're going and when you plan to return. If you're not back on time, rescuers will have an idea where to make their search.

6. Make sure your vehicle is in good winter driving condition. When you get ready to come home, a car that won't start can spoil your whole trip.

7. Drink plenty of liquids. Dehydration is more common in extreme cold. An adult, at rest, requires about 2 quarts of water daily. Up to 4 quarts are required for strenuous activity. There is a 25% loss of stamina when an adult loses $1^1/_2$ quarts of water. Avoid dehydration; simply drink as often as you feel thirsty.

8. If you're cold, eat something, drink something warm, and put on a cap. Most of the body's heat loss occurs thru the head.

9. Stay dry! When cloths get wet, they lose up to 90% of their insulating value. Wool is the exception. It retains a lot of its insulating value even when wet. So, if you're going to be out when it's both wet and cold, wool is your best bet. A waterproof windbreaker is very useful in helping to stay warm and dry.

Winter days can be very beautiful. To make sure you have an enjoyable outing: 1) be prepared;

2) take necessary precautions; and 3) respect nature's rules. If you follow these few simple rules, you will have a great Winter experience in your.......Wayne National Forest.

RANGER'S NOTEBOOK - Hypothermia is the number one killer of outdoor recreationists. It is a subnormal body temperature which, if not reversed, leads to mental and physical collapse. It is caused by exposure to cold, wet, and wind, thus causing body heat loss. A word of warning -- most cases of hypothermia occur in air temperatures between 30 and 50 degrees (F) above zero and during rainy weather; so, you can have problems not only in the Winter, but also in the Spring and Fall.

January 18, 1982 –

There are 187 million acres of National Forest land in the United States (including Puerto Rico). This includes land in every state except Iowa, Maryland, Delaware, New Jersey, Connecticut, Rhode Island, and Massachusetts. Ownership of these lands is vested in the over 220 million citizens of this country. That figures out to be just over 4/5 of an acre per person.

If you had your say, how would you want the Forest Service to manage your 4/5 of an acre?

Or, how would you want all of the 187 million acres of National Forest to be managed?

More realistically, how would you like to see your favorite National Forest or Forests managed? This could be the Wayne in Ohio, the Monongahela in West Virginia, the Hoosier in Indiana, or the Cherokee in Tennessee. Or you might have some particular interest in the Ocala in Florida, the Bitterroot in Montana, or the Allegheny in Pennsylvania.

The 187 million acres of National Forest represent a treasure of many things. The American people use these Forests for camping, hiking, fishing, mineral extraction, hunting, watersheds, grazing, timber, wilderness, wildlife and lots of other important activities.

Which, and how much, of the desired products and uses these lands will supply must be determined well ahead of time. Forests cannot be hurried. Thus, each National Forest is preparing a Land Management Plan which will outline how the Forest will be managed over a 10 year period. All plans will be completed by 1985.

The Wayne National Forest Plan is just starting and the target date for completion is 1983. We have sent out information packets with comment sheets that can be returned to us in a postage free envelope. If you have a concern in mind about how the Forest should be managed, please return your comments to us.

We are updating our mailing lists, and if by chance you did not receive the packet, just stop by the office in Reno or give us a call and we'll mail one to you. You can check the block to receive future mailings, or if you don't want to be on the list, we can remove your name also.

Over the next 2 years we'll keep you informed about what is happening with development of the Plan. We also request your ideas and opinions at any point in the planning process. We want the Plan to be responsive to the desires of the public. It's hard to please everyone, but we're going to give it our best shot. With your help and involvement, we will come up with an acceptable and well-rounded Plan. After all, it is your.......Wayne National Forest.

January 25, 1982 -

I've had several comments and questions concerning the recent newspaper article about the payments the Forest Service makes to the counties each year. Everyone either knew about this or was glad to hear about it.

As mentioned in the article, part of the payment is in-lieu-of taxes and part of the payment is based on the receipts taken in by the Wayne National Forest each year. Of the receipts, 25% is returned to the counties.

This includes money from timber sales, recreation, oil & gas activity, etc. As the number of oil & gas wells where the United States gets a royalty increases, so too, will the money to the counties increase because 25% will return to the local governments. I hope the amount keeps increasing because with the uncertain economic times ahead, I'm sure the counties will be able to put it to good uses.

One question I did get asked by a few people was this. "Okay, fine. The counties get the money, but is it used where it is most needed?" Well, a designated portion of the money must, by law, be used for schools and roads, while the rest can be used as the county officials see fit. Washington County, a few years back set up a system to ensure that the money goes where it is most needed -- and that is to Frontier School District.

The Frontier District, because of a lack of railroad access and other reasons, does not have the large industrial plants like Union Carbide, Ashland Oil, Elkem, etc., that some of the other Districts, such as Warren, have. These companies provide enormous amounts of tax monies to the School Districts in which they're located. Because of this, the County Commissioners, Frontier School District Superintendent, County Engineer, County Auditor, etc., agreed to the following distribution of National Forest money:

<u>Frontier School District</u> - 79 %

<u>Washington County Engineer</u> - 11%

with the remaining 10 percent divided

among the <u>6 Townships</u> that contain National Forest

land.

This system was started in 1977. So, from this year's

Washington County total of almost $25,000, the

Frontier District will receive nearly $20,000.

I might also add that another 10% of National Forest

receipts goes back to the various states for use by their

Departments of Transportation and Highway Departments

for upkeep on state roads that run through National Forests.

The past couple of years, I believe, the money has been used

on State Route 93 in Lawrence County.

If you have any questions regarding these payments, or

other matters, just drop us a note, give us a call (373-9055),

or stop by our office in Reno. If we don't know the answer,

we'll find it out for you.

RANGER'S NOTEBOOK - Everyone knows that trees

are used for lumber, furniture, pallets, and to make paper,

but what about the following: sugar and syrup, some

wallboards and insulation, musical instruments, smoking

pipes, charcoal, and fuel. Most of you probably knew about

those items also. Now it gets tougher! Which of the

following items either come from trees, or use a part of

the tree as an ingredient? See how many you get right. I'll give you the answer next week:
1) creosote, 2) alcohol, 3) tar, 4) dyes, 5) plastics, 6) vanilla flavoring, 7) oxygen to breathe, 8) chewing gum, 9) turpentine, 10) horseshoes, 11) shoe polish, 12) explosives, 13) pine oil, 14) crayons, 15) solder flux. I'll give you one hint. They all don't come from trees (or parts of trees).

Till next week, we hope you enjoy the outdoors and your ..... Wayne National Forest.

February 1, 1982 –

Recently we received the following news release from our Eastern Region Office in Milwaukee, Wisconsin --

Last year 423 people participated. Each in a special way.

Retirees, students, teachers, unemployed workers, sportsmen, Boy Scouts and Girl Scouts, and professionals combined to contribute $349,553 worth of work at little or no cost to the Eastern Region of the Forest Service, U.S. Department of Agriculture.

They were volunteers - men and women of all ages.

Since 1972, more and more people have been offering their services in several different ways. In the last seven years, 2,048 volunteers donated over $1 million worth of work.

Through their help, the Forest Service is able to accomplish projects that otherwise might be eliminated, postponed, or done irregularly. Their spirit of volunteerism is a prime example of what President Reagan is asking Americans to demonstrate.

Just what do volunteers do on some of the 14 National Forests in this Region? Whatever the needs are and whatever their abilities allow them to accomplish..

Perhaps the most visible are Campground Hosts. They work two to three hours a day for four weeks or more supplying information to campers and doing light clean-up work. Many others are working at less visible, but just as important jobs.

A college student on semester break maintained cross country ski trails and cleared blown down timber with handtools.

Boy Scouts and Eagle Scouts constructed two log dams to fulfill requirements for merit badges.

A husband and wife are preparing a slide/tape program on historical logging railroads within one of the Forests.

Another volunteer wrote a booklet and produced a map of locations of rare, threatened, and endangered plants.

Eight volunteers recruited by the American Hiking Society formed a trail construction crew for .3 miles of trail.

They were from New York, Illinois, Kentucky, and Minnesota.

A professional photographer took photos of activities on a Ranger District.

The Green Mountain Club in Vermont referred several volunteers to operate trail shelters in the summer.

A Ranger District even had a volunteer to recruit other volunteers. The list goes on and on.

Anyone wishing to share some knowledge or a skill can contact the Forest Supervisor's office of any of the 14 National Forests in the Eastern Region. Locally, contact us at 373-9055 or write to Wayne National Forest, Rt. 1, Marietta, OH 45750.

RANGER'S NOTEBOOK - Last week I listed several items that are either products of trees or by-products of processes involving trees. The list includes some items that amaze people. How did you do on last week's little quiz? Of the 15 items listed, all come from some part of a tree, except for #10, horseshoes. So, you can see how important trees and forests are, and what a wide variety of products come from them.

February 8, 1982 –

We were talking about Spring the other day, and about how glad we were that Winter was half over now. It brought to mind an old story I'd heard when I was a kid. I think you'll enjoy it.

As you all know the Appalachian Mountains, from our area all the way south to Georgia, can receive lots of snowfall and harsh weather conditions. In fact, it gets downright wicked at times. (Our northern neighbors in New England and elsewhere may not know this, but it's true nevertheless). Well, back to the story.

In pre-Civil War days, roads thru the mountains were few and far between. And what roads there were had to pass thru mountain gaps on the way to the low country. But there was mail service in those days, too. The mailmen travelled the old wagon roads and dirt turnpikes. Along these roads there were scattered inns, taverns, and coach houses.

Late one Fall a new mail carrier took over a mountain route. (I believe it was the one between Staunton, VA and Parkersburg, WV). While staying at an Inn one night, he became snowbound. Well, the story goes that after one or two failed attempts to cross the mountain, he came to enjoy the hospitality at the Inn so well that he decided to stay for the Winter. And it just kept snowing!

After a time the people on the other end of the mail route started to get impatient. Finally, they were able to get word out, along the coast, and on to Washington, D.C. Soon a tracer was sent out to locate the missing carrier, and more importantly, his mail. Thereupon he wrote a famous letter (which still hangs framed in Washington, D.C.), addressed to the Postmaster General of the United States.

The letter explained what had happened and it ended by saying, "If the floodgates of hell were to open, and it were to rain fire and brimstone for six straight weeks, it wouldn't melt all the snow on this mountain, so if those people want their blamed old mail, let them come and get it!"

This is a true story and I can believe every word of it. These Appalachian Mountains have spawned a lot of tales and folklore, many of which are among the most colorful in this country. It's a great heritage and I'm very proud of my "mountain roots".

February 15, 1982 -

Tree Facts

A full one-third of the United States is still forested. The densely populated states of New York and New Jersey are both more than half covered by trees.

Ohio is 27 percent forested. Much of this lies in the southeastern part of the State. Much of western and central Ohio, of course, is in farm land.

Of Ohio's forest land, 97% (or 6.9 million acres), is classified as commercial forest land. This is a 5.5% increase over 1968 figures.

Commercial forest land is land producing or capable of producing crops of industrial wood. This would be at least 20 cubic feet per acre per year.

In Ohio, the Oak-Hickory forest type is the most common, making up 62% of the commercial forest land.

Since 1968 in Ohio, the net growth of our forests has been 3 times greater than the removals.

The United States uses enough timber in one year to build a one-foot by twelve-foot boardwalk to the moon.

The nation's largest overall tree is the "General Sherman" Sequoia in California's Sequoia National Park. It measures 83 feet, 2 inches in diameter and is 275 feet tall. (Some trees are taller, but their diameters aren't that large. For instance, our tallest tree is a California redwood which is 362 feet tall).

Leaves have built-in thermostats to maintain the right temperature for photosynthesis. As the outside temperature rises, water from the leaf's pores evaporates, thus cooling it.

The thick, soft floor of a forest soaks up rainwater like a sponge. This water is filtered by the forest soil into clean lakes and rivers or into underground water tables that provide water for distant cities.

Most animals do not thrive in the middle of a thick, unmanaged forest. They prefer thinner forests and forest edges. Careful timbering and abundant wildlife are therefore often found together.

Some modern sawmills use television screens, electronic scanners, and computers to decide how a log should be cut. This up-to-date equipment can reduce waste by as much as 25%.

A tree in full leaf may take up to a ton of water from the soil in a day. This water may be delivered to the top of a 250 - foot redwood at the rate of 150 feet per hour on a hot, dry day. To do that in a building of similar height (25 stories) would require a powerful electric pump.

RANGER'S NOTEBOOK - Bob and Maxine Broedel, of Reno - Marietta Township, gave me a clipping which said that over the course of 50 years a tree is worth $196,250! - divided as follows:

air pollution control - $62,500

water recycling & humidity control - $37,500

oxygen - $31,250

soil benefits - $31,250

wildlife shelter - $31,250

protein in leaves & bark for wildlife food - $2,500.

These are direct benefits only. Considering the many indirect benefits the total would be much more.

February 22, 1982 –

BITS & PIECES

--Field & Stream Magazine gives the following definition of an "Unimproved Forest Service Campground" - a designation on National Forest maps to indicate a small swamp used for experimental breeding of killer mosquitoes. (There's a lot of truth in that statement some people will say).

-- About 2 years ago it was estimated that over 9 million dollars worth of minerals per year were taken from beneath the Wayne National Forest. On the Marietta Unit alone, there are over 350 active oil and gas wells.

--The Outer Continental Shelf, the offshore area bordering America, extends more than 250 miles to sea in some places and is 8,200 or more feet deep. Its total area is almost 6 times as large as oil-rich Texas. Geologists say this area may hold more than a third of all our oil still to be discovered and over a quarter of America's undiscovered natural gas.

--Oil companies pay the government for offshore leases to explore for oil & gas. In 1980 alone, this amounted to over 4 billion dollars worth of revenue. But the search for more domestic oil goes on and, as one historian noted, oil "is found in abundance only if a great many people are looking for it all at once in all sorts of unlikely places."

--What's a BTU? With all the emphasis on energy these days, we hear a lot about BTU's. It stands for British Thermal Unit and is the amount of heat energy needed to raise the temperature of one pound of water one degree Fahrenheit. Just a unit of measure, that's all it is.

— How about wildlife? Here was one of 1981's most interesting stories. A rare black-footed ferret was discovered in Wyoming. This was the Nation's most endangered mammal, and many people even believed it was extinct because none had been sighted since the early 1970's. Since the first sighting, two more ferrets have been observed in the same vicinity. Years ago, European ferrets were bred to hunt rabbits and kill rats.

--Fish and Wildlife Service research biologists report that eggshell thickness and reproduction are improving in eagles, osprey, and brown pelicans, and that the numbers of sharp-shinned hawks & Cooper's hawks are increasing dramatically. Researchers now agree that DDE, a persistent breakdown product of DDT, was responsible for eggshell thinning, reproductive failure, and population declines in the bird populations.

--In looking through an old publication here at the office, I noticed that as of 1972 Ohio held the national record for largest beech tree. The circumference was 18 feet, total height was 108 feet, and the crown spread measured 56 feet. What a tree!

March 1, 1982

Spring is emerging, the days are getting longer, February is behind us, and Easter is just around the corner.......vacation season will be here before long.

For their vacations many people like to visit the forest and park areas managed by the Federal Government. Some of these areas charge fees for entrance, use, and special recreation permits as authorized by the Federal Recreation Fee Program under the Land and Water Conservation Fund Act of 1965. Also, as part of the Federal Recreation Fee Program, the Golden Eagle Passport and the Golden Age Passport were established. Both of these can reduce the expense of visiting the parks and recreation areas, especially if several visits are planned or if a large family is involved.

The Golden Eagle Passport is for persons under 62 years of age. It is an annual entrance permit to parks, monuments, and recreation areas administered by the Federal Government. It admits the permit holder and a carload of accompanying people. Where entry is not by private car, the Golden Eagle Passport admits the permit holder and family group - parents, children, and spouse. The Golden Eagle Passport does not cover use fees, such as fees for camping, and other special use charges. It is valid for entrance fees only.

The Golden Eagle Passport costs $10 and is neither refundable nor transferable. It is good for one calendar year.

The Golden Age Passport is for persons 62 years of age and older. It is a free lifetime entrance permit to those parks, monuments, and recreation areas administered by the Federal Government which charge entrance fees. It also provides a 50 percent discount on Federal use fees charged for facilities and services such as camping, boat launching, parking, etc. The Golden Age Passport does not cover fees charged by private concessionaries.

The Golden Age Passport admits the permit holder and a carload of accompanying people. Where entry is not by private car, the Golden Age Passport admits the permit holder and his or her spouse and children.

You may only obtain a Golden Age Passport in person. Golden Age Passports are not available by mail.

At the time you obtain a Golden Age Passport in person, you must show proof of age. Proof of age may be a state driver's license showing your birth date, or birth certificate (Medicare cards are not acceptable because they are also issued to people under 62 years). If you have no proof of age, you must sign an affidavit attesting to your age.

The Golden Age Passport is available at most federally operated recreation areas where it is used. Thus, it may not be necessary to obtain the Passport before beginning a vacation trip.

The Golden Age or Golden Eagle Passport may be obtained by stopping at the Marietta Unit office on Rt. 7 in Reno. The mailing address is Rt. 1, Marietta, Ohio 45750. Our phone number is 373-9055. Remember that the Golden Age Passport must be obtained in person.

May you all have a wonderful, safe, and enjoyable vacation season in 1982.

March 8, 1982 -

Our geologist, Lynn Kantner, has put together a brief history of the petroleum industry in Southeastern Ohio. This is an important part of our local history, and comments, pictures, stories, etc. that will add to our historical file on oil and gas would be appreciated. So far this is what we have:

Ohio's petroleum industry started in southeastern Ohio. In 1814 near the town of South Olive in Noble

County, oil and gas were encountered in a well being drilled for brine. The well was considered a failure for brine, but the high gravity oil was used in lamps for lighting.

By 1819, oil was being produced in Washington County for lighting and medicinal uses. "Seneka Oil" was used as a rheumatism remedy. Another product containing petroleum, "Mexican Mustang," was a popular liniment.

Forty years later in 1859, the Drake well was drilled in Pennsylvania, while oil and gas leasing was active in Ohio. Commercial production was discovered along Duck Creek between Caldwell and Macksburg the following year. It was discovered that this oil was an excellent lubricant and the price skyrocketed to $28.00 a barrel.

Arlene Satterfield, up at Main Star in Newport, says that the price didn't come back to $28.00 a barrel until September 1979. If you're interested, somewhere in her files, Arlene has a list of oil prices from year one (in the oil business) till today.

Washington County was the scene of much of the early oil and gas exploration. As tools and drilling techniques improved, deeper holes were drilled. By 1900, wells all over southeastern Ohio were being drilled to depths of 2,000 feet.

In 1951, production in the Oriskany sand at 4,400 feet was discovered in the Marietta area. More recently new technology in drilling and completing techniques has enhanced production from various horizons in the Devonian shales between 3,000 and 4,000 feet in this same general area. Higher oil and gas prices have elevated known sub-economic reserves to economically recoverable status, increasing drilling activities in old and new fields throughout the state.

To date, only a few wells have been drilled to depths below 5,000 feet. The deepest rock sediments in Ohio are near Marietta. Approximately 13,000 feet of rock still remain virtually untested below 5,000 feet. The formations have reservoir characteristics suitable for the accumulation of gas and oil, and in other areas are productive.

RANGER'S NOTEBOOK -

Only about 10% of the minerals beneath the Wayne National Forest's Marietta Unit are owned by the government. The other 90% are privately owned. There are approximately 350 active wells on National Forest land in the Unit also. It was estimated a couple of years ago that over $9 million worth of minerals each year is removed from beneath the Wayne National Forest.

March 15, 1982 -

Spring is on the horizon. Though we may get another snow or two, we know it won't last very long. Spring brings thoughts of fishing, gardening, lawn work, and home repairs.

Last week was kind of unusual because I received three inquiries about the same tree pest -- the tent caterpillar. First, a question was asked during a program I presented at a Lion's Club meeting; second, we got a call on the same subject from a local school; and third, Marilyn Ortt, of the Marietta Tree Commission, called with some information that her group had concerning tent caterpillars.

I'm not an expert on forest insects and diseases, but I do know a little. And Marilyn Ortt provided me with some information on the eastern tent caterpillar by Richard Miller, an entomologist at Ohio State University.

In the past few years I'm sure most everyone has seen the white, silken-web nests of the tent caterpillar. Populations have been fairly high in our area. As you may have noticed, the favorite food of the caterpillar is the wild cherry or black cherry tree, followed by apple. However, they also feed on peach, plum, pear, rose, hawthorn, and other forest and shade trees.

What damage does the eastern tent caterpillar cause? Well, number one, for ornamental trees around homes, the webs that are constructed in the crotches of limbs and branches are very unsightly. Number two, since the caterpillars have huge appetites, they will often eat <u>all</u> the leaves off of the smaller and medium size trees. Number three, when they migrate in search of new food or new homes, they can sometimes be seen by the thousands covering sidewalks, roads, and even the sides of houses. In some areas this gets so bad that the highways are very slick and dangerous to drive on because of the squashed caterpillars.

Is this the extent of their damage? Basically, yes. While they will defoliate a tree, it's important to know that the tree will normally refoliate itself that same year. So the damage done is normally a one or two year period of stunted tree growth. Of course the tree is weakened and other diseases, insects, etc. could then come in. But the point is, if the caterpillars eat the leaves off your tree, don't cut it down thinking that it is dead, because it probably is not.

Larry Ehlers, Staff Forester - Forest Pest Management for the Division of Forestry - ODNR, tells me that the tent caterpillar is cyclic, peaking at about 5 to 7 year intervals. He says that natural enemies keep it under control, or else damage would be much worse.

Some natural enemies are parasites and predators, such as certain birds, beetles, and mice (when caterpillars crawl on the ground).

Since the eastern tent caterpillar normally doesn't kill trees, but is just more of a nuisance, the Marietta Tree Commission doesn't recommend chemical control. And it's probably not warranted for back yard control. This time of year, before the eggs start to hatch, just prune off any branches or twigs that have the clumps of egg mass on them. This should be done now, because soon the little caterpillars will hatch and bunch together to form webs. Even after webs appear on small branches and twigs, you could prune them off. Of course, you wouldn't want to do this on the large limbs, but perhaps there you could still destroy the webs by hand.

So, if you have any of the previously mentioned trees in your yard, and you anticipate tent caterpillar problems, right now is the time for action by pruning off the egg masses. And remember, if the leaves on your favorite backyard tree are eaten, your tree is not dead. It will normally recover.

March 29, 1982 –

Arbor Day. What is it? Many people know, many do not. Arbor Day is an important day in our nation's history. It's a day set aside to recognize the importance of trees in our lives, and a day especially devoted to the planting of trees.

Arbor Day began in Nebraska. Settlers moving west in the mid-1800's found vast, open plains that were treeless. Not only did they miss the trees of their eastern homes, but they also needed trees for other reasons -- for fruit orchards, for building materials, to reduce soil erosion (windbreaks), for fuel, and for shade. One pioneer family from Michigan, the J. Sterling Morton family, settled on 160 acres near Nebraska City. Soon flowers, shrubs, and trees were planted all over their property. Morton became a newspaper editor and later became involved in both State and Federal government. He was soon advocating that everyone plant trees. He realized that although the plains were treeless, they had a climate and soils very favorable to tree growth. His efforts were responsible for planting the area that became the great commercial orchard section of eastern Nebraska.

Morton proposed an annual tree planting day, to be known as Arbor Day; it was first observed in Nebraska on April 10, 1872. It was an enormous success, with over one million trees being planted in Nebraska on that day.

During the 1870's many other states began celebrating Arbor Day, and we even have a National Arbor Day -- the last Friday in April. Some southern states celebrate Arbor

Day as early as January or February, while some northern states celebrate it as late as May. Ohio first observed Arbor Day in 1882 and West Virginia in 1883. Ohio Arbor Day is celebrated on the last Friday in April, while West Virginia celebrates it on the second Friday in April.

Arbor Day became associated with schools, and over the years many thousands of school children have planted trees on this day. This year marks the 100th anniversary of Arbor Day celebrations in our schools. On April 27, 1882 school children helped plant trees in Eden Park in Cincinnati and to this day there has been a close association between schools and Arbor Day.

Sadly though, Arbor Day's importance in our country is fading. A surprising number of people don't even know what it is. As we've become "modernized" as a people, we've lost a lot of our contact with nature. The importance of soil, clean water, and clean air to our very lives is not widely understood.

My hope is that observances such as Arbor Day will somehow again gain the stature they deserve, that communities and civic groups will get involved in tree planting activities, and that our future will be all the better for it. For as J. Sterling Morton often said, "Other holidays repose upon the past -- Arbor Day proposes for the future."

April 5, 1982 –

Here are various items of interest I've collected over the past couple of months:

1) Fuelwood is now heating 14 million homes nationwide. About 2.5 percent of the nation's energy now comes from forest resources, compared with one percent in 1970. Forest product industries now supply 50% of their energy needs by burning their own wood wastes.

2) On National Forests, demand for fuelwood has risen 1100% since 1972, to more than 4 million cords a year.

3) If all wood waste, logging residue, dead trees, etc., could be used for energy, it would equal almost 1.7 billion barrels of oil. That's almost equal to our oil imports for 1981. Unfortunately, all of this vast unused resource is not now economically recoverable. Still, estimates are that by 1990 wood can provide about 8% of the nation's energy needs. This is certainly a significant amount. And since wood is a renewable resource, trees used for our energy needs can be grown for that purpose again.

4) Spring turkey hunting season is just around the corner. Dates are the last week in April and the first week in May. Those gobblers have been heard on recent mild mornings. Darrell Cline, avid turkey hunter from the New

Matamoras area, reports strong turkey populations that are steadily increasing their range.

5) Each year over 1400 collisions occur between birds and aircraft. This problem is serious around many airports. In 1981 a jet near Cincinnati hit a migrating loon, killing the co-pilot and injuring the pilot. And remember last Fall in Cleveland, when a collision between seagulls and an Air Force Thunderbird T-38 killed the commander of that famous flying team? A 4-pound duck struck by an airplane traveling at 300 miles per hour exerts almost 9 tons of force at its point of impact. When I was in the Air Force a T-38 training plane hit a bird on a glancing blow to the side of the canopy. The instructor pilot was in the back seat and was momentarily stunned, with several cuts and blood around his eyes. The student pilot in the front seat was not hurt much, but the canopy was shattered and communications was lost with the back seat. When the instructor pilot came to, his first thought was to eject from the aircraft, which he did, thinking that he was all alone since he couldn't see anyway. This left the student all alone. Rather than eject, since the controls were still working, he elected to return to base. With a little help from the ground, using visual signals, he was able to land safely. The pilot who parachuted was picked up safely, and though he had serious injuries, he did recover. Federal researchers and

wildlife biologists are currently studying ways to discourage birds from concentrating around airports. Projects center around biological control methods rather than the killing of birds. This could include such things as altering vegetation or changing drainage patterns to discourage nesting around airports.

RANGER'S NOTEBOOK – In 1980, 1.5 billion trees were planted in this country (two of that total are in my yard). This averages out to seven per every citizen. Annual reforestation on forest lands is about two million acres per year; 50% of those acres are owned by forest industries, while 15% occurs on National Forests.

April 19, 1982 –

Spring! What a wonderful time of year! It just makes you feel good to see plants blooming and to enjoy the warm days. And with daylight savings time beginning this weekend, we'll have more sunlight in the evenings and it'll really feel like Spring.

Right on schedule this Spring, as usual, was the blooming of the serviceberry
tree, with its pretty white flowers dotting the otherwise dormant hillsides. The "sarvus" has been in full bloom for several days now.

Just behind the sarvus in blooming comes the redbud. I noticed this past weekend that many of these beautiful pink shrubs are starting to show their color. Some of the fruit trees are starting to bloom, and the buckeye trees are in leaf, too. In another two weeks, just about every tree will be in leaf, except the oaks and a few others.

---- How about the other plants? Many wildflowers are in bloom, with others to follow very soon. And don't forget ramps! This tasty little edible plant brings joy to my heart each Spring. I get hungry just writing about it. The lily-like leaf (that's a tongue twister!) of the ramp is one of the first to emerge from the forest floor each Spring. They've been up for a month or more already. The bottom part of the ramp looks like a small, green onion, and it tastes similar (only better).

My two sons, Jeff & Brent, and I had a mess of ramps last week, with cornbread and beans. That's a meal fit for a king! Eating ecstasy! The best eating this side of heaven! And besides all that, we enjoyed the meal, too! My wife, Vicki, and daughter, Shannon, elected not to eat the ramps. That's okay – more for me!

Oh, I wish it was lunch time!

Last week I had an appointment with Mr. Newman Fitzsimmons of Ormet Corporation, located at Hannibal in Monroe County. He wanted to talk about and to look at a couple of items in the Wayne National Forest. On our second stop, along the side of a hill, I sat down and happened to notice some dark green, lily-like leaves protruding from the forest floor. You guessed it! Ramps. What a surprise! We left them alone and will keep the location secret, because it was just a small patch.

----All waterfowl hunters age 16 or older must purchase a duck stamp. These stamps cost $7.50 each and provide $15-16 million in revenue annually. This revenue goes toward the purchase of wetlands for feeding, nesting, resting, and wintering grounds for migratory waterfowl. Of course, these wetlands provide many other benefits to our nation -- they are vital links in many ecological chains. Nearly half of the nation's original 127 million acres of wetlands have already been drained or filled-in for developments, such as housing, businesses, agriculture, etc. Only 1.8 million acres of wetlands now exist as National Wildlife Refuges, set aside exclusively for wildlife (especially waterfowl).

Figures can be made to tell almost any story imaginable. Nevertheless, these numbers are somewhat alarming. While most of our natural resources are renewable, there is still a limit of damage beyond which recovery is doubtful. We are all part of an intricate ecosystem. Many of our actions affect plants and animals, and by so doing come back to affect us-often in ways we never imagined. Recent discoveries about "acid rain" in the Midwest and Northeast, and about the water problems in Florida cause concern and make us realize the negative effects man can have on his environment.

Wetlands are dwindling, our agricultural land base is shrinking, clean water is a rarity, and in some parts of the world thousands of acres of forests are falling to the bulldozer each week. While doomsday reports may be premature, we all must realize that natural systems are integral parts of our lives, and that man cannot survive apart from them. Harmful treatment of the environment generally results in harmful effects on mankind.

April 26, 1982 –

This past Winter I wrote my last historical sketch on the beginnings of the forestry profession in this country. I had gone from the 1600's all the way to 1875. Now, beginning in 1876, we see a rapid movement toward greater management of our forests.

The real beginning of forestry work by the Federal Government came just 100 years after the Declaration of Independence, when Congress in 1876 authorized the appointment of a special forestry agent. During the next quarter century, the forestry movement was mainly a campaign of public education. Toward the end of the period a forestry policy for government timberlands was established. Meanwhile, large-scale exploitation of timber resources continued.

1876 - A special agent, Dr. Franklin B. Hough, a physician, statistician, and naturalist of Lowville, N.Y., was appointed by Frederick Watts, U.S. Commissioner of Agriculture, to gather data on the supply and demand for timber and other forest products for the present and future; to report on means successfully used abroad to manage forests and means that may be used in this country to preserve and renew forests; and to investigate the influence of forests on climate.

A bill was introduced in Congress to ensure preservation of forests of the public domain adjacent to the sources of navigable rivers and other streams.

1877 - Congress granted its first appropriation, $6,000, to obtain information before establishing a Division of Forestry in the Department of Agriculture. Carl Schurz, German immigrant, statesman, and student, who became Secretary of the Interior in 1877, was among the first to propose and urge the establishment of federal forest reservations, and the scientific handling of forests. In his native Germany, forests were managed so that there was always a supply of wood. Trees were regularly and constantly replaced. He believed the same could be done in his adopted country.

Secretary Schurz and J.A. Williamson, a militant advocate of public forest control who had just become Commissioner of the General Land Office, completely reorganized the system of protecting and caring for public timberlands. District land registers and receivers were relieved of their timberland protection responsibilities. A force of special timber agents was organized and a drive was started against timber thievery and depredations on public lands. A new circular of instructions for timber agents was issued.

Connecticut set up a forest inquiry commission.

1877-83 - Three comprehensive reports by Dr. Hough were submitted to Congress.

1878 - The Free Timber Act and the Timber and Stone Act were passed by Congress. Until then there was no legal distinction between timberlands and other lands, and also no honest way to acquire public timberlands. The Free Timber Act gave the people of nine western States the right to cut timber at will on mineral lands both for domestic and mining purposes. The Timber and Stone Act authorized the sale of public land chiefly valuable for timber but unfit for agriculture and not previously offered for sale; the minimum price was to be $2.50 per acre and the maximum area sold to one person, association or corporation, 160 acres. The impractical and unenforceable provisions in these laws resulted in unprecedented fraud and opened the door wide to wholesale forest cutting and destruction. For example, in 1885, the Government sought to recover the value of 60 million board feet of high-grade lumber stolen from public forests by a single California company.

May 3, 1982 –

I have a couple of interesting items to talk about this week. First, it looks like our Little Muskingum YCC Camp, near Bloomfield, will be operating this Summer after all. This year, however, there's a slightly different twist.

Due to federal budget cuts and program eliminations, we knew we would have no Youth Conservation Corps this year, and it appeared highly unlikely that we would be able to utilize our existing camp facilities at all. This would have been a shame, since the investment at the camp runs several thousand dollars and includes bunkhouses, shower/toilet facilities, a kitchen/dining area, and complete water, sewer, and electric. But it takes time and money to open and operate a camp like this; and with the reductions we just were not going to be able to do it.

Then along came two people to our rescue -- Emerson Shimp, Washington County Extension Agent, and Emerson Henthorne, President of Hervida 4-H Camp, Inc. We talked about how we might somehow be able to utilize the camp and make it an asset to the community. We laid the groundwork, and with the help of our Ranger in Athens, Forest Service people at our main office in Indiana, and Extension Service people at their Regional and State Offices, an agreement was reached where Hervida 4-H, Inc. will operate the camp from May 1 – October 31, 1982. (The camp is not winterized, so this limits use to warmer months).

I am very pleased and grateful that Mr. Shimp and Mr. Henthorne are helping us to utilize the camp facilities, because heaven knows, they are busy enough running Camp Hervida. But they both have a sincere dedication to serving the youth and other organizations in our area.

Starting now, groups can reserve the camp for their use. Dates will go quickly, so set up your week or weekend as soon as possible. Youth groups, church groups, school groups, organizations --- all are welcome. Hervida 4-H has hired Ed and Maxine Payne of Route 2, Rinard Mills to run the camp and associated programs. Rates for overnight use will run in the neighborhood of $4 or $5 per person per day. If the camp isn't booked full, rates for day use (such as church picnics) may be available. Services provided will include outdoor education, recreation programs, canoeing, cooking, and other traditional camp activities.

For more information, or reservations, contact the Paynes at 1-614-865-2990, or Rt. 2, Box 74, Rinard Mills, Ohio 45774. You can also contact the County Extension Service at the Court House, 1-614-373-6623 or (toll free) 1-800-282-9700.

We urge you to take advantage of this opportunity to more fully enjoy your......Wayne National Forest.

Now for the second item. Last Thursday evening I had the honor of being invited to attend Frontier High School's All-Vocational Awards Banquet, as the guest of Mr. Calvin Martin and the Future Farmers of America. This is the second year in a row that I've attended, and I enjoy every minute of it. The students themselves put on the program and they do an excellent job. The FFA President, Tim Riggs, was Master of Ceremonies. He did a very good job, performing like a seasoned veteran. The FFA jointly sponsors the program with Future Homemakers of America and the Office Education Association. All three groups had parents and guests present; FHA President is Kaneta Eddy and OEA President is Kim Armstrong. All three groups put in a lot of hard work, along with their advisors --- Calvin Martin (FFA), Miss Buckton and Mrs. Brown (FHA), and Mrs. Voso and Miss West (OEA); and the hard work paid off with an excellent program.

I've worked with Calvin and the FFA group in locating certain tree species, tree and plant identification, and posters and pamphlets for use in class. They're a good group to work with --- very appreciative and interested in the outdoors. I sat with some of the students at the banquet and I don't want to forget to mention their names --- Rusty Van Noy, Jim Rogers, Jim Enges, Wayne Smith, and Kurt Satterfield.

May 10, 1982 –

Bits and Pieces from the Great Outdoors

1 -- Fifteen members of the Reno Christian Church had a nice hike on our River Trail last Saturday. And after the 4-mile hike, we had a very good picnic at the Leith Run Picnic Grounds. Though the weather looked ominous early that morning, it cleared off into a perfect day for hiking. Many wildflowers are out and most trees are in leaf, too. In addition to the Kincaid five, we had Bob and Maxine Broedel; Bob and Martha Given; Mary, Ann, and Mary Lisa Simmons; and Jan, Jean, and Ellen West. Spring is a beautiful time to get out and enjoy your Wayne National Forest.

2 -- A few months back I reported the sighting of the first black-footed ferret in 10 years. Many had thought the animal was extinct. Now comes a report that a wildlife biologist in Wyoming has found <u>at least</u> 22 more of them. Researchers believe the species may be making a comeback. Let's all hope so.

3 -- Fishing picked up dramatically last week. I talked to some guys fishing on the Ohio River above Willow Island and they were having good luck. So far, I've heard of sauger, smallmouth and largemouth bass, catfish, bluegill, and crappie being caught, some in good numbers. An article that came through the office last month said that America's appetite for fish was on the increase and has been so for several years. In 1980, the U.S. imported 54% of its seafood. These imports added 5% to the Nation's trade deficit. Because of this, new efforts are being undertaken to increase our food-fish production. One method is by encouraging more farmers to grow fish, such as catfish, salmon, and trout, for market.

4 -- Some of the bans on pesticides seem to be paying off now. Since DDT was banned 10 years ago, several bird species, including brown pelicans and bald eagles, have recovered to where they are now repopulating former habitats. Evidently the chemical residues are fading. As you will recall the reproductive systems of certain birds were affected by the pesticide. In particular, it caused eggshell

thinning. Bald eagles had just about vanished in the East and the Great Lakes area by the late 1960's, due to feeding heavily on fish in which DDT residues had accumulated. Florida's eagle population, which had been reduced 90% in the 1950's, has made a nearly complete recovery. All this should be good news, not only for bird enthusiasts, but everyone.

5 -- As you've no doubt heard, the 17-year locusts (or cicadas) are coming. Sometime this month, as if by magic, they will emerge from the soil after 17 years. That's a long time to be in the ground! Most of eastern Ohio will be affected this year. The main damage they cause is when the female makes deep slits in the twigs of trees to lay her eggs. Most damage occurs to young fruit and shade trees, which cannot withstand this as well as older and larger trees.

Once the eggs hatch, in about 6 weeks, young nymphs drop to the ground ,burrow into the soil, and attach themselves to a root where they can get sap from the plant. This can cause "tree decline," a general loss of vigor for the tree. A few weeks before these "locusts" emerge this year, you'll see either little dirt chimneys or several holes in the ground. I noticed some out back this weekend. The holes are about $1/4$ inch round.

Once the nymphs crawl out of the ground, they will be mature adults with wings in 24 hours. You can see the skins they shed hanging on trees or on the ground.

Soon, you'll hear their monotonous, droning sound. Egg laying will follow in a week to 10 days. If you have planted young fruit or shade trees this Spring, it might be wise to cover them with something like cheesecloth or mosquito netting to protect them from the egg-laying female. This should be done <u>before</u> May 25th. If you go with chemical control, use sevin, and follow instructions carefully. Spray when the cicadas start singing, which is prior to egg-laying. Be thinking now about how to protect your trees and shrubs from this interesting, but sometimes destructive, insect that lives above ground for only 3 months and underground for 16 3/4 years.

<u>May 17, 1982 –</u>

How about the beautiful weather we've been having lately! It sure makes you forget about Winter fast, doesn't it? All in all though, we could definitely use some rain. What a difference a year makes. Last April and May we had so much rain farmers couldn't get their crops planted. This year the crops are planted, but not growing much.

If you've been in the woods lately, you've no doubt seen many wildflowers in bloom. Others will follow in the weeks ahead, but the Spring flowers are beautiful right now. Here are a few that I've noticed lately in the Wayne National Forest:

1) <u>Mayapple</u> - This is a good one to start with because it is perhaps our best known and most abundant wildflower. It seems like it grows everywhere, but it actually prefers rich soil. The umbrella-like leaves hide a pretty, white flower in the fork of the two-leaved mayapple. The flowerless stems are terminated by only one large leaf. Later on, about July, a small, edible "apple" will appear and ripen. To tell you the truth though, the "apples" don't taste that great!

2) <u>Wild Blue Phlox</u> - This is sometimes locally referred to as Wild Sweet William. It is fairly abundant in southeastern Ohio, with its light purple or bluish flowers visible for quite a distance. I've seen it blooming in rocky woods and along mountain stream banks.

3) <u>Fire Pink</u> - Here's one of my favorites! The narrow, deeply-red colored petals are double-toothed at each end. Their brilliant color is hard to miss, growing most often in shaly, drier soils. The English people called this flower Catchfly, because the stems are covered with sticky hairs to which insects become attached.

4) <u>Trillium</u> - I think you can find at least 3 different types of trilliums in the Wayne National Forest. The <u>large-flowered or white trillium</u> is the largest, and

perhaps most plentiful, growing in large patches in rich woodlands. The white flowers will turn pink with age. The painted trillium has somewhat smaller leaves and petals than the white trillium. Though also white in color, it is characterized by a crimson blaze in the center. The red trillium is easy to recognize by its maroon or purple flower. The name trillium comes from Latin and means three, referring to the fact that all parts of the plant, including leaves and petals, are arranged in threes.

5) Spring Larkspur - Sometimes called Dwarf Larkspur, these bright violet- blue flowers belong to the buttercup family. Growing most often in rich woods, you can sometimes find white-flowered plants, too.

6) Jack-in-the-Pulpit - This flower definitely grows in rich woods, being hard to find in any other place. The name refers to the appearance of the "Jack", or preacher, peering out from his canopied pulpit. The color is mainly dark purple, but with pale green color appearing in spots or stripes. The bulb-like base was highly prized as food by the Indians, hence the name Indian-Turnip.

7) Common Blue Violet - Let's not forget this pretty little flower that seems to grow all over the place. It's a favorite of children everywhere, and the flowers can be used to make a tasty, and pretty, light-blue jelly. (My wife and I have made that jelly a couple of times.) The

petals are in 5's and are sometimes white or yellow in color.

I hope I've mentioned your favorite Spring wildflower. There are so many that I could only mention a few of the most common. Be on the lookout and you'll be amazed at how many wildflowers grow in the Wayne National Forest.

May 24, 1982 –

Would your group, school, or organization like to spend a week or so camping at our Little Muskingum YCC Camp, in the heart of the Wayne National Forest? If so, call me at 373-9055; or call Emerson Shimp at the Washington County Extension Office - 373-6623; or call Ed and Maxine Payne at Bloomfield - 865-2990.

In the past two years we've had many requests for such use of the camp, and we've had many more inquiries as to whether groups could use the facilities. At that time the answer was no. Now, however, thanks to Washington County Extension Service and Camp Hervida 4-H, Inc., we are able to offer interested groups the chance to enjoy and use this outdoor setting.

Through a special agreement, Camp Hervida will run the camp for us from May thru October. The next step is to get interested groups to reserve and use the facilities, because, without use, the camp will be shut back down! We figure that a minimum of 30 days use between now and October is required to make it worth opening the camp. Why? Because there are some costs involved such as casualty insurance, personal liability insurance, days spent planning and organizing, opening & closing costs, electrical and water work to be done, cleaning up the seven buildings, and several other items, also.

For me, it would be easy just to shut back down, but I surely don't want to do that! Why? Because we've got a nice facility there, near Bloomfield on the banks of the Little Muskingum River, where churches, schools, and other groups could go for outings, environmental education sessions, and outdoor recreation. And there has been a certain amount of clamor in the past year over "What are you going to do with the camp now that there is no longer a summer YCC program?" Interest seems to be there for using the facilities.

Now, what do we need? Very simple! We need groups to reserve the facilities and utilize them for at least 30 days this summer. Reservations need to be received in the Extension Office, or by the Payne's in the next couple of weeks or the program just is not going to fly. Camp Hervida has to have some commitment before they can justify hiring a caretaker and setting up summer programs.

The camp setting offers an endless number of unique opportunities --- proximity to the Wayne National Forest, access to the Little Muskingum River with its excellent canoeing and fishing, outdoor education sessions, and perhaps best of all, a quiet, serene setting for your group to enjoy a few days of "getting away from it all."

So the time is here to speak now or forever hold your peace. We must have some commitment or else scrap the idea. Rates are very good --- in the neighborhood of $3 or $4 per person per night; food service is also available; and even day use rates may be possible for something around $30 or so per group.

Call one of the previously listed phone numbers today to make your reservations, and take advantage of this excellent opportunity to enjoy your......Wayne National Forest.

P.S. The camp will not be rented during deer hunting season, for obvious reasons.

June 7, 1982 –

The Pileated Woodpecker is a somewhat "shy" bird that lives in the forest, far away from people. Right? Wrong! I saw one in town the other day. As a matter of fact it was in my backyard, about 20 feet away from where I was standing on my side porch.

It was about 7:45 a.m. and I had gone outside to water some plants. Suddenly I heard a loud whack, whack, whack! It sounded like someone in the backyard beating on my yellow-poplar tree with a ball peen hammer. In other words it <u>was</u> loud! I peeked around the side of the house and to my surprise, there it was --- a pileated woodpecker. It startled me, too, because if you've never seen one of these birds up close, you can't believe how large they are. This thing was well over a foot long, probably about 1 $^1/_2$ feet total. And, of course, I immediately noticed the bright red crest that seemed to cover most of its head --- I was no more than 20 feet away from this bird, and here it was whacking away at the side of my tree as if it was trying to punch a hole through to the other side. Bam, bam, bam! I sneaked back in the side door to tell Vicki, so I'd have some proof that I wasn't dreaming. We must have watched the woodpecker for a couple of minutes. It's a beautiful bird and the thing that grabs your attention, other than the red crest, is its size --- much larger than the normal backyard fare of robins, cardinals, sparrows, and quite a bit larger than a pigeon.

I had never seen a pileated woodpecker close enough to actually study what it looked like. I had seen a few in the woods, but they were always at quite a distance, and usually flying away. This bird is very shy, which still makes me wonder what it was doing in town. The answer, though, lies in the base of my yellow-poplar tree. There's a hole there that was crawling with carpenter ants, one of the pileated's favorite foods. How the bird found this tree in the middle of a residential area, I'll never know. They usually return to the same tree again and again, so I suppose it's been back --- we just haven't seen it (and it doesn't look like I have many ants on the tree anymore either).

Usually the pileated woodpecker would be found in large, wooded areas, such as the Wayne National Forest. It will sometimes search old stumps for insects, and will also use the tall, dead snags found in the forest. This bird became very rare at one time, but has made a comeback in recent years. A relative, the ivory-billed woodpecker in the Southeastern U.S., is thought by most experts to be extinct.

It was quite a thrill to see this beautiful, large bird as close as we did. There are still many outdoor photographers waiting to get close enough for a good shot of a pileated woodpecker (and wouldn't you know it, my camera was ready, but I was out of film). The pileated woodpecker is just one of the many interesting, beautiful, and beneficial birds that inhabits the Wayne National Forest.

RANGER'S NOTEBOOK - Without birds, I think insects would devour us. There's a balance in nature that we all need to know about. Birds eat many, many insects each day, often consuming more than their own body weight! The other evening I watched a half dozen birds "feasting" on our 17-year locusts or cicadas. They were catching the cicadas in midair, as they flew from tree to tree; and they didn't miss many ---very efficient! Think about the value of birds in keeping insect populations under control.

June 14, 1982 –

Today's column was written several years ago by forester Lacy Johnson, who is now retired from the Forest Service and living in Devola. I'm sure you'll enjoy reading it......

Within the past week a strange sight has appeared out along the Little Muskingum River and State Road 26, near the entrance to the Wayne National Forest. About three acres of land is decorated with small colored flags fluttering in the breeze. Spaced out in rows, the flags look like Flanders Field or markings for a new cemetery. Actually though, this is not a cemetery, but a birthplace. The birthplace is of an orchard, but no ordinary kind of fruit will be grown. It is a seed tree orchard established to produce black walnut seeds (fruit) for reforestation of walnut on parts of the Wayne National Forest.

Forest tree seed orchards are relatively new in this country. The purpose of the orchard is to produce the finest quality trees genetically possible. The original seeds came from selected trees in the forest, which have superior characteristics of form, growth, height and vigor. In this particular orchard the seeds came from 60 different walnut trees scattered from New York to Tennessee. After the walnut seeds were collected, they were planted and given a start as seedlings in the Vallonia forest tree nursery in Indiana.

Special attention and care will be required, through the years, of the trees in this newly established orchard. Each tree has been carefully recorded and identified on a master plan. Weed control will be necessary each year until the trees are well established. In following years trees will be thinned, leaving only the very best trees for final crop trees to supply walnut seeds for the Wayne National Forest.

Forestry is farming, in a sense. The difference from regular farming is that planting, cultivating and harvesting takes place over longer intervals. Many of the things the farmer does such as selection of seed and methods of cultivation are as important to the forester as to the farmer.

By the time the final selected crop trees are fully mature this forester will be retired, but not hobbling around on a cane, I hope. The younger foresters who take care of the trees will have each tree tagged and named. Maybe they will get to know each tree so well they will put names on them, like Pete, Charlie, Bill or Jake. Maybe by then I'll have grandchildren and can tell them, "That tree is Jim, I planted him back in the Spring of '75."

June 28, 1982 –

Connie Potts of Route 1, Woodsfield, recently attended the week-long Ohio Forestry Association Camp near Mansfield, Ohio. So did 160 other high school students from all over Ohio.

I served as one of the eight instructors for the camp. We taught classes in tree identification, forest ecology, silviculture, and forest products. There were also many other activities, including campfires, a firefighting demonstration, volleyball, and sing-alongs.

This was as fine a group of high-schoolers as you could ever be associated with. To begin with, they had to have an interest in forestry or the outdoors in order to come to camp. Tuition was $125 and almost every camper went out and got a sponsor to cover the cost. Connie was sponsored by the Monroe Soil & Water Conservation District.

The Ohio Forestry Association has been sponsoring this camp for many years. It's a very fine camp, well-run and organized. I urge any interested high school students, age 15-18, to check with their guidance counselors at school next year for more information about the camp. If you're interested in forestry or any related field, this is the camp to attend. It's both educational and fun.

If you want to know more about it, just ask Connie Potts of Woodsfield, or give me a call here at the office.

---- Most readers, I'm sure, have heard of Westvaco Corporation. They're one of the country's leading pulp and paper companies. A couple of weeks ago we had a chance to view some of the operations on their Parkersburg District Woodlands, which includes land in Wood, Wirt, and Ritchie Counties across the river in West Virginia, and also substantial acreage in Washington County, Ohio, mostly back in behind Belpre.

They are mainly set up to provide pine pulpwood to their paper mill in Luke, Maryland. We were able to see some of their pine plantations, and to discuss maintenance and care of them. Also, we viewed their whole-tree chipping operation, and visited a young stand of pitch-loblolly pine hybrid trees. These trees grow fast, like loblolly pine, and are able to withstand cold and snow, like pitch pine. They hold a lot of promise for the future production of trees for the paper industry.

We also had a chance to see the impact of oil and gas activities on Westvaco's land. One stop was the well in Ritchie County, drilled last year, which initially produced 1000 barrels of oil per day. The minerals were held privately, not by Westvaco.

----The Spring Turkey Season yielded 631 gobblers this year, from 20 different counties. This was a new record, surpassing last year's total by over 50 birds. The wildlife biologists say the turkey population is steadily increasing, and is very healthy. Vinton was the top county with 127 birds taken; Hocking County was second with 86; Washington County was 11th with 22 birds, and Monroe County 17th with 7 taken. I heard one report that a gobbler was taken with a bow in Pike County. This is a rare feat, because the turkey is so wily and cunning that it is next to impossible to get close enough for a good shot with a bow. The re-establishment of the wild turkey in Ohio over the last 20 years or so, is a success story whose full credit must go to the ODNR-Division of Wildlife.

July 12, 1982 –

What was going on in the Reynolds Run/Davis Run area this weekend anyway? You may have seen a bunch of green or camouflaged trucks up there, or noticed many people running around in green uniforms. And if you were near enough you may have heard quite a bit of noise, too -- like machine guns and M-16's (no live ammo though, just blanks).

What happened was that the U.S. Army Reserve, Company D, 463d Heavy Combat Engineer Battalion was holding a weekend simulated war games exercise. More specifically, according to Sgt. Les Fortner, it was an offensive infantry tactics maneuver. The location was in the Wayne National Forest, out off the end of Township Road #417 in Independence Township and extending on south into Newport Township. There are quite a few acres of National Forest land in that area that enabled them to have room for their drill. Sgt. Fortner said it worked out fine, the mission was a success, and all training objectives were met.

The U.S. Department of Agriculture which includes the country's National Forests, has entered into many Cooperative Agreements with the various military branches for the purposes of training and maintaining defense readiness. In the past several years there have been many maneuvers in Wayne National Forest, mostly in the Athens area. This may have been the first one on our Marietta Unit. It worked out well though, because it was close to the Reserve Headquarters in Reno, and also fairly close to another participating Unit out of New Martinsville, W.Va.

We're glad to cooperate with these people in helping to maintain and improve our defense capabilities. And it's a pleasure to deal with a professional like Sgt. Fortner, who was easy to work with and very well organized.

So, next time you see army trucks and lots of soldiers storming out over Wayne National Forest, chances are they're not repelling an invasion of our southeastern Ohio oil fields, but it's probably just Company D of the 463d having another training exercise. (at least I hope that's all it is!)

On another note.... When the permit with the County Extension Service fell through for use of the YCC Camp facilities, we thought we'd have to keep the camp in mothballs for another year. But that proved to be untrue. Calvary Community Church of Belpre, which had planned to rent the facilities off the Extension Service for a couple of weeks anyway, decided to apply for a permit from us. They have recently complied with all insurance requirements, etc., and have the camp under permit through October,

1982. So now the facilities won't have to set vacant all summer.

-- One final note, a sad one, too. Walt Wagner, who had been working here since 1977, retired last Friday. Walt's services for the Wayne National Forest, which included land appraisals, right-of-way work, and oil & gas work, will be sorely missed. Over the years Walt had worked on National Forests in Oregon, West Virginia, Indiana, and Ohio. Walt and his family will continue to live in the Marietta area, where he will "take a well-deserved vacation, get caught up on work around home, and probably get into the appraisal business." We hate to see Walt go, but wish him the best for the future.

July 26, 1982 –

It's always enjoyable to get out and talk to youth groups about the Wayne National Forest and about the profession of forestry in general. Young people are very attentive and interested in talking about the outdoors. It's a perfect time to get them to understand the importance of our outdoor environment, how to enjoy it, and how to take care of it wisely.

This month we talked to a group of kids attending a church camp, led by Mrs. Andra Lewellyn. They were mainly 3rd-6th graders. We had interesting discussions about Wayne National Forest; how forests benefit man;

products that come from trees; campfire safety; and littering. We had a very good discussion.

Then last week we were out at Camp Hervida to present a class on forestry to the intermediate 4-H group. Emerson Shimp and Beth Hahn were running an excellent camp. The 4-H'ers that went with me on the forestry hike were keenly aware of the benefits of forests to man and wildlife. We went into a little more detail about forest ecosystems. While discussing tree growth, we had a chance to take an increment boring of a few trees to measure their age. The kids were very interested in this, as we were able to count the rings of the tree from the small increment core that I removed from the tree.

Sometimes we're so busy with work that it's difficult to schedule presentations to everyone and all groups that request them. But we try to work something out if at all possible, or schedule it for a later time. We appreciate the interest of people who want to know more about their......Wayne National Forest.

To change the subject, here's an interesting and encouraging note. This year has been designated the "Bicentennial Year of the Bald Eagle" and, almost as if on cue, the bird seems to be making a comeback.

In the 50's and 60's the use of DDT and other pesticides got to the point where eggshell thinning was occurring in eagles and other birds. This caused nesting failures. Also, many people were shooting eagles (some states even had bounties on them) because they mistakenly thought they were a threat to poultry and young livestock.

Populations of bald eagles became endangered or threatened almost everywhere, particularly in the Southeast and the Mid-Atlantic states. Last year, however, a nest was active in Georgia for the first time since 1970. An eagle pair nested in Arkansas on the White River for the first time since 1950. Florida's population is increasing. Eagles have been seen along the Potomac River and in New England. The Great Lakes states, whose populations have remained higher than the Southeast, are also increasing in numbers.

Joint research studies, rehabilitation of injured birds, various surveys, cleaning up the environment, re-introducing young birds into the wild -- all of these, plus more have contributed to turning around the decline in our bald eagle population. The key to keeping healthy populations of bald eagles, or any other animal, is maintaining adequate, clean, and suitable habitats.

August 2, 1982 –

BITS AND PIECES

Concerning the recent newspaper article about firewood, we've had a number of people either stop by the office or call in. Keep these points in mind:

1) You must stop at the office to pick up a permit. This is so we can go over the rules with you, make sure you know the location of the firewood area, and so you can sign the permit.

2) You must have the permit with you while you're cutting firewood. Areas will be spot-checked by Forest Service personnel. Anyone cutting without a permit is in violation of federal law and will be fined.

3) The limit is 5 cords per year, and the firewood is for home use only. It is not to be sold or traded. This is so there will be plenty for everyone.

4) In most areas you have to fell the trees yourself, though in some cases they are on the ground. In either case, you will have to buck and limb the trees yourself. It is not stacked or piled for your use. Some areas require substantial effort to get to the wood; some may even require a 4-wheel drive vehicle, or occasionally a farm tractor. In other places you may have to carry wood 100 or 200 feet to your vehicle. The point is, gathering the firewood may be time-consuming and very hard work. It may also take more or different

equipment than you have. Think about these things before you decide to go get some firewood.

5) Stay in the marked area. People cutting trees outside the area will be prosecuted. Taking advantage of the free offer of firewood or continuously violating the rules means that the area will be shut down permanently.

6) Cut only during dry weather. Do not cut during or immediately after a rain. This causes damage to roads, especially rutting, pot holes, and erosion. Firewood access roads will be monitored. If they are being damaged, we will close the areas. This means you must plan your cutting, and do it several months ahead of your firewood need this winter. (You should let your wood air dry for 3-6 months before use anyway).

7) Cut your stumps as low as possible to the ground, preferably 12 inches or less. All roads and ditches must be kept open. Don't leave limbs and tops in ditches or on roads. These cause access problems and also plug up culverts and ditches, thereby creating water runoff problems. If a tree must be felled into the road, just be sure to cut it all up and remove it before you leave.

8) Be careful! Take your time; rest frequently. Make sure your equipment is in good working condition and

that you know how to operate it properly. Wear standard safety equipment.

9) Always check for any electric, telephone, or gas lines in the area. If you have doubts or questions about the safety of cutting a certain tree, then don't cut it. It is not worth the risk.

Cutting firewood is not all fun and games. You must be prepared to be safe, and you must be prepared for hard work. If you're not, perhaps buying wood from someone is your best bet. You can still save money on your gas or electric bill by doing this. However, if you're prepared to accept the challenge, know what you're in for, and have a need for some firewood, we will definitely try to help you find some.

August 16, 1982 –

What great weather we've had during the past week -- warm, sunny days, not too hot and nice cool evenings. I could stand another month of this kind of weather.

This week we'll cover several short subjects:

1)   First, our clerk/typist since 1968, Doris Thomas, recently retired. Many of you had grown accustomed to seeing her in the past. She decided to take her retirement and enjoy the good life for awhile.

We'll all miss Doris and I'm sure everyone wishes her the best of luck in retirement.

2)	Pam Conley, who has been helping out for the past year under the Young Adult Conservation Corps, is working during August to replace Doris until our new clerk starts. Pam has done an excellent job in her year's training, and we're sure she's ready for a permanent job somewhere now. Replacing Doris will be Connie Morris, of Woodsfield, who has worked the past 3 years in Monroe County for the Switzerland of Ohio School District.

3)	Back to the weather. The recent cool snap puts you in the mind of squirrel hunting season. I've noticed quite a few squirrels this summer. It seems rabbits are all over the place, too. The same goes for grouse -- we jump grouse all the time while working in the woods. And the deer and turkey populations both seem to be on the rise. It should be a good Fall for hunters.

4)	It was reported last year that hunters and fishermen spent a record $455 million on licenses, tags, permits, and stamps. The Fish and Wildlife Service reported that nationwide there were over 16 million hunting license holders and almost 30 million fishing license holders. These figures are low, too, because many senior citizens, persons under 16 years of age, the disabled, and certain military personnel are not required to have licenses. Also, most coastal States don't require licenses for saltwater fishing. Much of the revenue from license sales is used by the states to help conduct their fish and wildlife management and restoration programs. The Fish and Wildlife Service apportions money to the States according to the number of license holders in each State. Under this program up to 75% of the cost of a project is reimbursed. Ohio stands about 16th on the list of total hunting licenses issued in this country. Pennsylvania was first last year, Michigan was second, and Texas was third. For fishing licenses, Ohio was 10th, while California was first, Texas was second, and Michigan was third. Hunting and fishing in Ohio contribute a lot to the economy and are very popular types of outdoor recreation.

RANGER'S NOTEBOOK - Ohioans are known as "Buckeyes" and this is the "Buckeye State." The buckeye tree abounds in Ohio. The nut from the tree has a close resemblance to the eye of a buck deer. The Indians had a name for "eye of the buck deer;" it was "Hetuch." In a future column I'll write about the famous buckeye tree.

August 23, 1982 –

Perhaps no other state tree in this country is as well-known or is as well-associated with its State as is the Ohio buckeye. Ohio is the Buckeye State; Ohioans are known as "Buckeyes"; and the Ohio State University Buckeyes are known everywhere, especially on the football field.

Where did this name "Buckeye" come from anyway? Well, we know for sure that it comes partly from the fact that there are many, many buckeye trees native to Ohio (two different species, in fact; but more on that in a minute). The buckeye nut is a dark purplish brown color, except for a small light colored patch on each one. This nut strongly resembles the "eye of a buck deer." Because of this resemblance, the Indians called the tree "Hetuch," their name for eye of a buck deer, or "buck-eye." This explains the name of the tree; but how did an entire state and its people come to be known by this Indian name?

It could have started in Marietta in 1788, according to one tale. The first court in the Northwest Territory was established that year. To mark the occasion a grand procession was held in Campus Martius Hall, headed by the High Sheriff, Colonel Ebenezer Sproat. Sproat was a huge man, and marching with his sword drawn, he made a great impression on everyone. The Indians, in admiration of this man and his appearance, began calling him "Hetuch," an honor not given lightly because of their great respect for the buck deer. Well, as is often the case, this nickname stuck and Colonel Sproat soon became known far and wide as "Big Buckeye". Others eventually gained this nickname too, and as Ohio gained statehood and more national prominence, Ohioans came to be known as "Buckeyes".

During the campaign of William Henry Harrison, who was the first president elected from Ohio in 1840, buckeye walking sticks and buckeye wood cabins came to be used as two of his symbols. This seemed to finalize in this country's mind that Ohioans were buckeyes. It wasn't, however, until 1953 that the State Legislature officially adopted the Buckeye as the state tree.

Two species of buckeye are native to Ohio - the Ohio buckeye, found throughout most of the state and the yellow buckeye, confined mostly to southern Ohio, primarily in the Ohio River drainage. The two species are similar and difficult to tell apart. Here's the easiest way: the nut hull of the Ohio buckeye is prickly, while that of the yellow buckeye is smooth. The nut of both looks the same - smooth, with the characteristic color and "eye."

Often confused with these buckeyes is the horse chestnut tree, which is in the same genus as the other two, but is an ornamental that has been widely planted since its introduction from its native Greece. Here's one easy way to identify it: the horse chestnut generally has seven leaflets, while the buckeyes usually have five. These leaflets, 4 to 6 inches long, are attached at a common point to a long stem. The buckeye tree is one of the first trees to "leaf out" in the Spring. Of the two buckeyes the yellow buckeye grows tallest, often reaching 70 - 80 or more feet, while the Ohio buckeye seldom grows over 50 feet tall.

Buckeye wood is not particularly important or valuable, but it is easily worked and resists splitting. Perhaps the most important uses are for artificial limbs and for woodenware. The nut is bitter and, if eaten in large amounts, is poisonous to man. Some animals, especially squirrels, feed on the nuts, but only if better food is not readily available. Some people carry a buckeye nut around as a good luck charm, instead of a rabbit's foot or other similar item.

One thing is certain no matter what you know about the tree. If you're an Ohioan, you're a Buckeye, and you have a heritage to be proud of.

August 30, 1982 –

Fall hunting season is just around the corner. These recent cool days and nights make the squirrel hunters anxious to start. They'll have to wait until September 9 though. Squirrel season starts on that date and runs through November 13 on private lands and through December 18 on public lands.

From all indications this season should be as good as the last couple, which fall into the average category. The good squirrel hunter who knows what he's doing, where to go, and does some advance scouting should have little trouble taking his limit of squirrels. Don't forget that the daily limit is four squirrels, with a possession limit of eight after the first day. Hunting hours are one-half hour before sunrise to one-half hour after sunset.

The guys at work here have noticed squirrels starting to move the last few days, triggered perhaps by the cool weather or the days starting to shorten. The squirrels are apparently looking for that really good hickory tree as a food source.

I've got a couple of favorite areas that I'll be trying out soon - one near Rinard Mills and one near Newport. Most wildlife biologists rate eastern or southeastern Ohio as having the best squirrel hunting in the state, which makes sense especially for gray squirrels. The gray squirrel prefers heavily forested land and large trees, which serve a dual purpose of dens and a food source. Southeastern Ohio, according to the most recent statewide timber inventory, is the only section of Ohio which has more forest land than non-forest land. Thus, the gray squirrel loves it here.

The larger fox squirrel is not as abundant as the gray squirrel here, but if you know where to go you can still bag some. Fox squirrels prefer to hang out along the edge of woods where they can slip into nearby corn or grain fields to eat. Division of Wildlife people tell me that the fields and woodlots of western and northwestern Ohio have many, many fox squirrels. Locally, try along the edges of the larger creeks and rivers where there are trees to provide dens, and nearby fields for food. Floating the Muskingum, Little Muskingum, or Duck Creek should provide some shots at fox squirrels, with maybe an added bonus of wood ducks later on when the season comes in.

Most of my squirrel hunting success has come in the early morning or late afternoon, when their most active feeding seems to occur. Mid-afternoon may produce a few squirrels, but this is their resting time. Getting up early is well worth it if you can look forward to sitting down to a meal of squirrel, biscuits, and gravy. Um-umh! That's a meal that's hard to beat.

Get your gun ready; squirrel season is just around the corner. If you don't have a good place to hunt, there are lots of places in the Wayne National Forest. Just

stop into our office in Reno for a map. Good luck this
season!

September 6, 1982 –

Driving along Interstate 77 last weekend, I noticed an
awful large number of dead animals, including one deer,
which had apparently been hit by vehicles. I remember
reading not too long ago that many more animals are killed
each year by cars and trucks than by hunters. One of the
western states reports several times more antelopes killed
by vehicles than by hunters. I believe the same holds true
for animals around here, especially for smaller animals like
rabbits; and you certainly see a lot of skunks, raccoons, and
opossums alongside the roads.

The opossum (let's call it "possum") population,
however, doesn't seem to be hurting too badly. This animal
produces several offspring each year, and over the last
century or two is one of the few animals that has
substantially increased its range naturally, not having to rely
upon the complex restocking methods required by other
animals. In fact, the possum, which during our early colonial
days was reportedly only found in the South, can be found
as far north as Canada and as far west as California. It has
probably spread as far north as it can though, because even

in Ohio possums are commonly found with black, brittle ears - the victims of frostbite.

Why has the possum increased its range when most animals have found reduced habitat? The answer probably lies, quite literally, in your garbage can. The possum can, and will, eat almost anything, which has led the animal to follow the garbage dumps and refuse piles of man - almost anywhere. Though the animal can be found in remote areas, it is quite possibly more abundant around the edges of urban areas.

The possum is a marsupial - an animal having a pouch in which to feed and carry its young. It's related to the kangaroo. The possum has two litters per year of 10-15 young, which are so small when born you can put them in a spoon. A possum lives normally only a couple of years and weighs between 5 and 12 pounds. They feed primarily at night, usually on carrion, or dead animals. They also eat insects, fruit, and birds' eggs among other things. A possum den may be any place where it can stay dry and hide from its enemies. It might live in a deserted den of another animal, a hole in a tree, or an old building foundation, and prefers to be near a source of water.

How about some possum folklore? The animal would rather run than fight and can climb trees in an instant. Even if cornered, it rarely fights, but will often roll over, open its mouth, and play "possum". Kids be careful, though, because with its mouth full of sharp teeth it can inflict a painful and severe wound. There's more folklore than just playing dead however. In our early days it was said that the possum's long rat-like tail could cure a cough, end constipation, and even hasten child deliveries for women in labor.

The Aztecs of Mexico used possum tails to make salve and tea, and considered the animal to be very good eating. The legends aren't all good, however. It was said that one of the worst things a Cherokee Indian could call another was a word which translated into "possum manure". The Catawba Indians had a word referring to the possum, which translated into, "He who slobbers much fluid".

Oh well. Legend aside, the possum remains one of the most widespread, and therefore important, animals in the United States.

RANGER'S NOTEBOOK - Have you seen the bumper stickers that say, "Eat More Possum?" They are put out by the Possum Growers and Breeders Association of America. The Association, headquartered in Clanton, Alabama, claims a membership of over 40,000.

September 13, 1982 –

BITS & PIECES

1 - As you may have read, there is a new District Ranger for the Athens Ranger District of the Wayne National Forest (this includes both the Marietta Unit and the Athens Unit). The new Ranger is Gary Coleman, who is moving to Athens from a previous assignment in the Eastern Regional Office at Milwaukee, Wisconsin. Gary is originally from Pennsylvania, is married with two children, and graduated from Penn State University. He's looking forward to his new job and anticipates meeting a lot of people in both Monroe and Washington Counties. Gary replaces Bob Joens, who transferred to the Superior National Forest in Minnesota.

2 - We were pleased to participate as an exhibitor this year in the Washington County Fair. It's a very nice fair, well organized and run by the Fair Board and all the committees. We had a good spot under the grandstand and were pleased to answer many questions about the Wayne National Forest. If you had other questions, or didn't get a chance to stop by the exhibit, don't hesitate to call us or drop by the office here in Reno. Our phone number is 373-9055.

3 - I had another interesting evening last Thursday as I was invited to present a program at the meeting of

the Civitan Club. David Grimes asked me to talk about National Forests in general, and about the Wayne National Forest in particular. We watched a movie on the role of National Forests and the complexities of managing a Forest. Then we had a real interesting question and answer session lasting about 15 minutes. If your group or club would be interested in a program, we'll try our best to work you in sometime. Just give us a call to make arrangements.

4 - Speaking of which -- we've also been invited to participate in the Founders Day parade at New Matamoras on Saturday, September 25th. This should be a very nice parade and a big weekend for New Matamoras. We made a request to have "Smokey the Bear" join us in the parade and if all goes as planned, he'll be there to wave to all the kids.

5 - And one other thing we'll be involved in next month is the Second Annual Washington County Energy and Conservation Fair at the Joint Vocational School. Tom Daggett, at the JVS, and Emerson Shimp, County Extension Agent, are putting together an interesting day of exhibits, seminars, and demonstrations. The Fair is Saturday, October 23rd from 10:00 A.M. - 4:00 P.M. Hope to see you there.

6 - A special thanks to two groups this year that helped us complete our hiking trail maintenance as

Volunteers in the National Forest. John Hutchison, of New Matamoras, and his Troop #250 completed maintenance on the Ohio View Trail, as part of an eagle project for one of the Scouts. The trail is 8 miles long. With our reduced budgets this year we would have been hard pressed to do the work ourselves, but thanks to Troop 250 the work was done anyway. Also, two students from Debbie Lazorik's Outdoor Recreation class at Marietta College spent a couple of days helping us maintain the $3^1/_2$ mile long River Trail. This was part of a project they were doing for her class and the help was surely appreciated.

7 - As our budgets continue to get cut, any Volunteer help we can get is appreciated. One organization that does more than its share is the Southeastern Ohio Chapter of the National Wild Turkey Federation. These folks are always willing and able to do habitat improvement and maintenance projects that will benefit the local turkey population. Turkeys are fairly abundant in several sections of the Wayne National Forest.

September 20, 1982 –

I recently wrote an article entitled, "Wayne National Forest: Model of Multiple Use." The article appeared in the Journal of Forestry magazine, which goes out to over 20,000 professional foresters. Here is the article. I hope you enjoy it.

WAYNE NATIONAL FOREST – MODEL OF MULTIPLE USE

The Wayne National Forest is one of the newest and smallest members of the National Forest System. Flourishing on reclaimed land and abandoned farms, this youngster is a study in renewing natural resources.

Some 4 million people live within a 100-mile radius of the Wayne, and the forest is quickly becoming a very popular and valuable piece of public land. With a total population of nearly 11 million, Ohio has only $1^1/_2$ percent of its land in public ownership. The importance of the state's one national forest can readily be seen.

History, Acquisition, and Administration

The Wayne was officially established in 1951 on lands tucked away in the rugged Appalachian foothills of southeastern Ohio.

Revolutionary War hero "Mad" Anthony Wayne, after whom the forest is named, negotiated an Indian treaty in 1795 in the densely forested territory. Settlers soon arrived to cut roads through the woods and to clear and burn fields for farming.

The nineteenth century saw extensive timber harvesting, and oil and gas drilling began in 1819. Oil was produced for local lighting and medicinal purposes 40 years before the first commercial well was drilled in Pennsylvania.

Strip mining in this coal-rich area was sparked by World War II, and left thousands of acres scarred by spoil banks.

The first tract for the Wayne was acquired by purchase in the mid-'30s, when depression families were eager to sell marginal farmlands. Acquisition continued through the 1940s and 1950s, and with the official opening on October 1, 1951, management began on 100,000 acres. The Wayne now contains over 176,000 acres located in 11 counties. It is made up of three units, separated geographically - the Ironton, the Athens, and the Marietta Units. For supervisory purposes, there are two districts, the Ironton and the Athens, with the latter including the Marietta unit. Within the boundaries of the three units, approximately 20 percent of the land is national forest with the balance in state or private ownership. For administration, the Wayne is linked with the Hoosier National Forest in Indiana.

In recent years, old mine lands around Athens and Ironton have been reclaimed by the Wayne National Forest in conjunction with the USDI Office of Surface Mining. Additional acquisitions are planned.

Forest Types

Ohio forests are generally grouped with the central hardwoods, but the southeastern region also has species associated with the Appalachian Mountains. However, black cherry, northern red oak, basswood, and hemlock make up less than 10 percent of the forest. The oak-hickory group, with white, red, black, scarlet, and chestnut oak and several species of hickory, comprises over 70 percent. On better sites, and especially in moist coves, yellow-poplar is common, often occurring in pure stands. Pines form 10-15 percent of the forest and are generally less than 45 years old. Many abandoned fields were planted with white, red, shortleaf, and Virginia pine. Native stands of white, shortleaf, pitch, and the dominant Virginia pine also occur. Other common species are red maple, beech, white ash, black walnut, sycamore, sugar maple, aspen, black locust, elm, and, of course, Ohio buckeye.

Products

Ohio is no longer heavily forested. Pasture and cropland make up more than 50 percent of the land base. Just 27 percent of the state's 26 million acres remains in forest. Of this acreage, 6 percent is in public ownership, 10 percent is held by industry, and 84 percent is in nonindustrial private tracts. The southeast is the only part of the state with more forest than non-forest land.

Nevertheless, Ohio does produce high-quality sawtimber and wood fiber to support paper mills and other industries. Veneer-quality white oak, red oak, and black walnut are still grown and harvested. Mature yellow-poplar grows on many of the better sites. Nearly 55 percent of the Wayne is in sawtimber stands, about 30 percent is in pole timber, with the remainder in seedlings and saplings. Though the Wayne is of secondary importance to Ohio's total wood market, it is very important to local mills and loggers. Loaded log trucks are a familiar sight on forest roads. A high-lead cable logging system is currently in operation on the Ironton unit. It is being used on steep ground, not suited to conventional skidding, and is one of only a few such systems operating in the East.

- continued next week -

September 27, 1982 –

(Continued from last week)

Part 2

of:

Wayne National Forest -

Model of Multiple Use

Recreation and Wildlife

Ohio's small public-land base places recreation and wildlife habitat areas in short supply. The metropolitan areas of Cleveland, Akron-Canton, Toledo, Cincinnati, Dayton, and Columbus, not to mention Detroit, Pittsburgh-Wheeling, and Charleston-Huntington, are all within a two to four-hour drive of the national forest. Increasing numbers of citizens from these cities are discovering the Wayne for hunting, hiking, fishing, camping, and sightseeing.

The large Lake Vesuvius facility north of Ironton offers trails, campgrounds, and a reconstructed Vesuvius Furnace. This chimney, used for smelting iron ore, was built in 1833 and operated until 1906. The Hanging Rock region, west of Ironton along the Ohio River, also has a long history. During the Civil War, it was one of only three places in the world capable of producing high-quality iron needed for heavy cannon.

Another major recreation area includes a campground on the reservoir at Burr Oak Cove north of Athens.

Sightseeing tours follow scenic and historic country roads through the forest. Marietta, first permanent settlement in the Northwest Territory, was founded by Revolutionary War soldiers who had received land in lieu of pay. Spring and fall color tours are planned to cross a number of authentic covered bridges in the area.

The Ohio River forms almost the entire southern boundary of the Marietta unit, and picnicking and boating are popular, especially at Leith Run picnic grounds and boat launch area. Streams, such as the Little Muskingum, offer miles of serene, undisturbed canoeing.

The wildlife program consists of habitat management for deer, turkey, grouse, waterfowl, and many nongame species. Wildlife work is implemented through proper planning and operation of the timber management program. The deer population is healthy and herd size is increasing. Grouse hunting is so good that national magazines have rated the Wayne better than certain Lake States areas. Turkey populations, on the rise since the 1960s, now number several thousand. As a result of pollution control, the Ohio River once again offers excellent fishing. Bass tournaments are held in the popular Willow Island Pool above Marietta. Streams like Symmes Creek and the Little Muskingum River yield smallmouth bass, crappie, and muskie. Rather than traveling to far-off places, local hunters, fishermen, bird watchers, and outdoor enthusiasts are coming to the Wayne.

Until recently, a free firewood program issued several hundred permits each year, but in 1981 this figure jumped to well over 4,000. The rapid increase in firewood demand is taxing the forest's ability to maintain supply. Firewood is plentiful, but access becomes a problem. Among management alternatives being considered are limiting the number of permits, increasing requirements for permits, or charging for firewood.

Minerals

The biggest impact on the forest since 1978 has been a rapid increase in drilling for oil and gas wells. Most of the minerals beneath the Wayne National Forest are privately owned. The energy shortage, with accompanying oil and gas price increases, created a boom atmosphere for drillers and developers, particularly on the Athens and Marietta units.

Over the last several years, Ohio has been listed among the leading states for new wells drilled; Washington County ranks in the top three counties in the nation. Much of this activity has been on or near the Wayne. Three years ago, more than $9 million worth of minerals (oil, gas, and some coal) was removed from beneath the Athens district alone, and the figure is higher today. Nearly 1,000 wells exist on the 176,000 acres of the forest. Some are 50 to 100 years old and still producing, while perhaps one-third have been drilled since 1977. Royalty payments accruing to the federal treasury can be expected to rise steadily as more government-owned mineral rights are leased and drilling begins.

Several Wayne employees spend a large part of their time coordinating and monitoring oil and gas production. The work ranges from helping with initial location and layout of well sites, roads, and pipelines all the way to inspections for post drilling reclamation. Oil and gas production has proved to be compatible with forest management, provided that operations are properly planned and adequate precautions are taken to protect other resources.

Come and See

The Wayne National Forest is a model of multiple-use activity. From providing outdoor recreation to producing high-quality hardwood timber, from reforesting disturbed watersheds to meeting the nation's energy needs, the Wayne is a gem in southeastern Ohio.

October 4, 1982 –

Congratulations to Frontier High School's FFA Forestry Field Team! They finished 4th in last weekend's Paul Bunyan Show competition at Hocking Technical College in Nelsonville. The competition among the several FFA groups included tree identification, tree measurements, and computing timber volumes. The Paul Bunyan Show is an excellent annual event put on by the Ohio Forestry Association. It includes the FFA competition, exhibits, field events (like chopping, sawing, and splitting), and other demonstrations of modern forestry equipment and techniques.

In addition to the very fine 4th place team finish by Frontier High School, one member of their team, Steve Joy of Newport, finished in 4th place in the individual standings. This is an excellent finish among a group of over 100 competitors from throughout Ohio. Steve is in the 10th grade and figures to do even better next time around. Congratulations Steve!

John Kerr, Forestry Technician here at the office, worked with Calvin Martin, FFA advisor at the school, to set up an area where the students could practice their tree identification and measurements. The students practiced several times and the practice paid off with their high scores at the Paul Bunyan Show.

The leaves are changing color, the nights are certainly cooler, the air has that definite feel that Fall is here. With Fall comes hunting season, one last chance for good fishing before Winter arrives, and an excellent opportunity to view animals and birds of all kinds as they prepare for Winter.

I noticed a flock of geese the other day flying in straight-line formation, rather than a V-formation. I heard them honking for a time before I finally spotted them -- 7 nice Canada geese. I'm not sure if they were moving through, or if they were some of the group that hangs out around these parts. In either case, I always get a thrill out of watching them in flight, with their long slender necks pointing the way.

Squirrel hunters are reporting good success in most areas. Last week on the Wayne National Forest in Grandview Township, I saw 3 nice gray squirrels and noticed several places with a lot of hickory cuttings.

Grouse hunters should enjoy another successful year. Populations seem to be still very high. October 8th is opening day for grouse and the season runs through February 28. We jumped 4 grouse last Wednesday while checking out a work project on the Forest. Seems like every time we go out, we jump grouse. It's a fine game bird and as good eating as any game in the woods.

Deer seem to be moving quite a bit, too. It won't be long before we start to notice buck rubs and scrapes. With days getting shorter, and after a frost or two, those bucks will really start being active.

Let's not forget fishing. After those hot summer doldrums, the water temperatures are now falling and our rivers and streams will offer some very fine fishing.

Last October and November I had a couple of nice outings for smallmouth bass on the Little Muskingum River. And how about the fishermen who specialize in catfish. My neighbor, Larry Weber, and his Dad, Frank (of Marietta), are two experts when it comes to fishing for mudcats. Larry said August was a terrible month for the most part, but after mid-September things started to pick up considerably, including catching an 18-pound mudcat last week. I went with him a couple of nights later and within about 25 minutes of each other he pulled in a 12-pounder and a 4-pounder. He filets these smaller fish, and after his wife Elaine puts the finishing touch on them, you couldn't ask for a better tasting meal. Frank caught a 23-pounder a while back, and between them they've caught over 300 lbs. of mudcats this year.

Whatever your pleasure may be -- fishing, hunting, bird watching, or hiking -- Fall is an excellent time to get out and enjoy the great outdoors, and especially your.......Wayne National Forest.

October 18, 1982 -

BITS & PIECES

1) More good news from the recent Paul Bunyan Show, which was held at Hocking Technical College over

in Nelsonville. Last week we reported on Frontier High School's fine effort and I read in the paper about Marietta High School's accomplishments, too. Now Terry Schafer, Forestry Instructor at the Washington County Joint Vocational School, calls me to tell about his team's high finish in the lumber grading contest. He reports that the JVS lumber grading team of senior Don Travis and junior Loren Ewing finished in 3rd place. Also, Travis came in 2nd in the individual lumber grading competition. There were over 100 competitors from all around Ohio in the Paul Bunyan competition. The teams from this area seem to have done exceptionally well this year. Congratulations to all of them!!

2) Part of the New Matamoras Founders Day celebration was a BASS fishing tournament held on September 25 at the Willow Island Pool of the Ohio River. This pool is gaining in popularity as one of the better fishing stretches of the river. The launch point for the tournament contestants was at the Wayne National Forest's Leith Run Boat Ramp and Picnic Area. Tournament Director Ralph Dunn of New Matamoras was well pleased with the turn out for this year's contest and believes it will get bigger and bigger as it develops into an annual event. Ralph said, "There were 21 boats entered and about half of them registered fish. The

biggest fish checked in was a largemouth bass weighing nearly 3 pounds." Of course, almost all boats landed fish, but many smaller ones were put back in the water immediately. Most of the fish caught were largemouths, but there were some smallmouths, Kentucky spotteds, and even 2 muskies. (One of the muskies had a tag on it from the West Virginia Department of Natural Resources). Now that water temperatures have decreased substantially since September, the fishing has really picked up. In fact, the next couple of months can offer some of the best fishing of the entire year.

3) A word about firewood. Remember, the Wayne National Forest does offer free permits for firewood. There are some rules, however. The limit is 5 cords per year (which is plenty for this area). It must be used for home heating. The wood cannot be sold or traded to anyone. Anyone caught stealing or selling firewood from one of these "free-use" areas will be prosecuted. You must stop by our office in Reno to get your permit, and you must carry the permit with you while cutting wood. If you don't, and we ask to see it, you can be fined. Now, the areas that we have set up still contain plenty of wood. It's true that the easiest and perhaps best firewood has already been cut. Who cut it? The ones who were well organized, planned ahead, and cut it last Spring and Summer like they should have. So if

you have to carry your <u>free</u> firewood further than you'd like, or you don't get the exact kind of wood you want, don't come in here complaining. Blame yourself! Remember, the early bird gets the worm. Next summer, get an early start yourself and be prepared. Your firewood should air dry a minimum of 3 months before you burn it anyway, and preferably 6 months.

October 25, 1982 –

Last week I received some interesting and timely information from an old friend of mine -- Don Pfitzer, who works with the U.S. Fish and Wildlife Service in Atlanta, Georgia. Don and I met when I worked on the Chattahoochee National Forest in the mountains of north Georgia. We were both members of the Georgia Outdoor Writers Association, and generally had a lot to talk about, as we were both employed by the federal government. Of course, as you've no doubt read in my past columns, the Wayne National Forest (and the 153 other National Forests, too) is part of the Department of Agriculture, while the Fish and Wildlife Service (and the National Parks and Bureau of Land Management) is part of the Department of the Interior.

I thought you might be interested in the information Don sent me because it has to do with the fish and wildlife restoration funds and money sent to states for hunter education programs. This year $82 million total was sent to the States for these uses, including $54 million for wildlife restoration, $16 million for fish restoration, and $12 million for hunter education programs. The money is authorized by the Dingell-Johnson Act and the Pittman-Robertson Act, which are laws named after the congressmen who introduced the legislation.

What I like about this money is that it comes from hunters and fishermen themselves. Excise taxes are collected on purchases of hunting and fishing equipment. Much of the fish and wildlife habitat improvement work in this country, including acquisition and protection of key wetlands, lakes, and rivers, has been financed by hunters and fishermen.

The wildlife restoration and hunter education programs come from an 11% excise tax on sporting arms and ammunition, a 10% tax on pistols and revolvers, and an 11% tax on certain archery equipment. State distribution of money is determined by the number of hunting license holders and the land area of each State. Uses include acquisition of prime habitats, development and management of habitat areas, and scientific research. The hunter education money is allocated according to the relative population of each State.

The fish restoration money comes from a 10% tax on fishing rods, reels, creels, and artificial baits, lures, and flies. Distribution is determined according to the number of fishing license holders and the land area of each state, including coastal and Great Lakes waters. The fish money is spent for purchase of key areas, construction and rehabilitation of lakes, development of facilities and fisherman access sites, and fisheries research.

Ohio's share of this year's $82 million dollars is nearly $2 million. Hunters and fishermen can be proud that they have helped finance these vital programs, which have helped non-game, as well as game species. The key to any animal population is availability of suitable habitat. And in addition to hunters and fishermen, these programs have added to the enjoyment of millions of hikers, birdwatchers, campers, boaters, and canoeists. It is estimated that sportsmen have contributed $5 billion for these restoration programs in the last 50 years.

As explained in previous articles, the Wayne National Forest provides key habitat for many game and non-game animals, and the Forest also provides over 176,000 acres in southeastern Ohio for the enjoyment of hunters, fishermen, and other outdoor enthusiasts. The state of Ohio manages the animals and sets the regulations, and the Wayne works with them in habitat management. This joint effort provides countless hours of enjoyment midst the beauty of your.......Wayne National Forest.

November 1, 1982 –

I received an interesting note in the mail that told how landscaping can cut fuel costs. Of course we all know the value of trees for firewood, timber, wildlife food and habitat, beauty, etc. But a lot of times we overlook the value of trees and shrubs in helping reduce heating and cooling bills. Just how much your bills are reduced depends on your choice of plants and where you locate them. Side benefits may also be reducing noise and air pollution and increasing the value of your property.

How many times have you seen a home built out on a barren knoll or in an open field? Or how about the small woodlot that is often cleared completely of trees before the house is built? These aren't always the cases, but you frequently see them nowadays. An unprotected home loses much more heat on a cold, windy day than on an equally cold, still day. Well-located trees and shrubs can intercept the wind and cut your heat loss. You see this around many of the old farm houses where pines are planted as windbreaks. The penetrating power of the wind itself and heat loss caused by conduction through the walls and roof can both be reduced by windbreaks and foundation plantings. One-third to two-thirds of your home's heat loss can often be prevented this way.

One study in Nebraska showed where a house, maintaining a 70° F inside temperature, used 23% less fuel if protected by a windbreak. An all electric home in South Dakota used 34% less kilowatt-hours during the Winter because of windbreaks than an identical home that was more exposed to the elements.

In addition to reducing the force of the wind, windbreaks can make it more comfortable to be outside working around your house by reducing the wind chill impact. Evergreen trees generally make the best windbreaks, and 2 to 5-row windbreaks generally are best in stopping the wind and creating dead air space around your home. A study of a 3-row windbreak of 25-foot tall trees (evergreens) indicated less wind chill index than exposed homes. At wind speeds of 10 miles per hour, the reduction was 17° F wind chill index; at wind speeds of 20 mph, the reduction was 31° F. A side benefit to this is reducing the amount of snow that blows and drifts against your house.

The amount of money saved by a windbreak around a home will vary depending on the climate of the area, location of the home, and what the house is built of. A well-weatherized home with adequate ventilation, caulking, and weather stripping won't benefit from windbreaks nearly as much as a poorly weatherized house. Still there can be substantial savings.

I have some additional information on windbreaks, foundation plantings, and planting trees for both heat and shade. I will give a few more hints concerning these items next week. **(continued)**

November 8, 1982 –

Trees and Shrubs Can Cut Fuel Costs – Part II

Last week we discussed the value of trees used as windbreakers around your home. Today let's talk about foundation plantings and shade control.

Trees and shrubs planted close to buildings can substantially reduce wind currents that chill the outside surfaces of your home. These foundation plantings also create a "dead" air space which slows the escape of heat from the building. And, of course, air infiltration around the foundation would be reduced, too. Evergreen trees and shrubs are thicker than deciduous plants and are usually more effective as foundation plantings. To be most effective, the evergreens should be planted close together to form a tight barrier against air movement. In the summer, this dead air space helps insulate the foundation from hot outside air, thus reducing some of your air conditioning needs.

Another consideration around your home is planting trees to control solar radiation. Deciduous trees are often best for this. In the Summer they will shade your home from direct rays of the sun, if planted on the southern exposure. During Winter after the leaves have fallen, the sun's rays come through and help warm the house.

Trees with full crowns, such as American elm and sugar maple have long been favorites for Summer shading. (Of course the recent problem with Dutch elm disease has reduced the desirability of the elm tree). Evergreens generally have a more cone-shaped crown than hardwood trees, and thus provide less summer shade on walls and roofs; and since they don't shed leaves, if they're planted in the wrong location, they could shield the house from the sun's warmth during Winter.

Trees provide maximum shade when planted in groups beside your house. However, a roof need not be totally shaded to achieve measurable results. One study showed that air conditioning costs could be reduced effectively as long as a roof averaged 20% or more shade for the entire day. Another study showed that an

212

8° Fahrenheit difference between shaded and unshaded wall surfaces was equivalent to a 30% increase in insulating value for the shaded wall. (And it is quite common to find 8° F differences between shaded and unshaded building surfaces.)

There are a lot of things to consider when planning for windbreaks, foundation plantings, and shade or solar heat control around your home. Perhaps the most important thing to keep in mind is that it may take several years for the trees or shrubs to grow large enough to begin having the desired effects on the home. But once they reach the desired size, and if planted correctly, they will add beauty to your home and help cut fuel costs for many years to come.

For assistance you can contact any local nursery, your county extension agent, the Soil Conservation Service, or perhaps the local extension forester.

November 22, 1982 –

TO BURN OR NOT TO BURN

The use of fire in the forests of the United States has come full cycle. The early settlers found Indians using fire to clear brush in certain areas, to maintain some fields for farming purposes, and to improve wildlife habitat for hunting in other locations. The settlers adopted these practices, plus they cleared and burned literally millions of acres for farming, grazing, and homesteading.

As was often the case, the white man went to extremes in his zeal to "conquer" the land, rather than to live in harmony with it as the Indians had done. Many fires throughout the 1800's and early 1900's that were set to clear a piece of land, escaped control and became rampant wildfires. Many areas were burned year after year after year until the humus layer of soil was destroyed along with most of the vegetation, thus leaving nothing but exposed, bare soil. The result--massive erosion and millions of acres of nonproductive forest land, especially in the South and the Lake States.

Though it was recognized that fire could be beneficial in certain cases, foresters began to advocate keeping fire out of all forests because of the destruction that was occurring. And thus the forester's role, as far as fire was concerned, became that of keeping fires out of forests, or at least limiting their size and putting them out as quickly as possible. The symbol of Smokey Bear saying, "Only you can prevent forest fires" became the best known symbol in this country. And thru Smokey's campaign and the efforts of foresters over the course of several decades, we have limited the destruction of forest fires and re-established millions of acres of productive forest lands.

However, it has long been recognized by forest scientists that fire can have many positive effects, too. In the past several years, foresters have increased their use of controlled or prescribed fires to accomplish such jobs as insect and disease control, wildlife habitat improvement, preparing areas for seeding or planting, reducing hazardous fuel before it builds up to a dangerous level, managing understory hardwoods, and even to clear brush and enhance the appearance around certain campgrounds and recreation areas. But this is all done under carefully controlled and monitored conditions! It's done under strict supervision, in specific locations, for definite reasons, and always under a particular set of weather conditions. If it's too dry, or too windy, or the wind is coming from the wrong direction, the prescribed fire will be postponed until conditions are just right.

Around here the main uses of prescribed fire would be to improve wildlife habitat and to try to influence the species of trees coming back after a timber cut. We have some studies in progress to determine if controlled fires can help us get young oak seedlings to come back in certain areas. In some places we have a lack of oak regeneration, with sites being taken over primarily by red maple and yellow poplar. Perhaps fires under certain weather conditions can kill these two thin-barked species and allow the slower growing oaks to have a better chance to grow.

Wildlife biologists and hunters have long known the value of fire in helping maintain and create open areas for animals, and also to stimulate the growth of some browse and food plants. Most berry-producing shrubs can be revitalized by the use of prescribed fire. Locally, the berries and browse are good for songbirds, deer, and grouse; and turkeys find abundant insect food in many of the open areas.

What foresters have found is this: Controlled fires are beneficial for not only forests, but for wildlife and other reasons, too. But, uncontrolled wildfires can still be a threat to our forests and other resources; so, they are put out as fast as possible. In short, you can't just say fire is good or fire is bad. It depends on the type of fire -- whether or not it is controlled or running wild.

November 29, 1982 --

Jeff peered around the edge of the big white pine tree, trying his best to see whether or not the deer had antlers. But it was just so thick and brushy that he couldn't get a good line of vision to the deer which stood about 50 yards away.

The thick fog had hung heavy in the air just as daylight slowly crept across the ridgetop allowing Jeff and I to see the woods below us. Jeff is my oldest son and this was his first real deer hunt. This year he was going with me to watch and learn, and the plan is that next year he'll bag his first buck. (Only time will tell whether or not our plan works).

It was opening day and we were both excited. Still, it felt and looked like rain to me. I knew a cold rain would make things miserable for Jeff on his first deer hunt, so I had my fingers crossed, hoping for a decent day.

We were hunting on the Wayne National Forest in Monroe County, near Graysville, in excellent deer woods. We had gone into the forest about 20 minutes before daybreak and were eagerly awaiting the scene to clear up.

Jeff and I had sat down beside a fallen yellow-poplar tree and we were watching an area of about half an acre below us. There were deer trails running around the side of the hill, crossing a small creek, and going through a "saddle" between two spur ridges. Several trails came together in the saddle. It was a perfect crossing for deer going from one ridge to another. As far as deer paths go, this was an interstate highway. There was fresh deer sign everywhere -- trails, droppings, buck rubs, scrapes. From our vantage point, about three-fourths of the way up the slope, we would be sure to see any deer that came through that area. Or so we thought!

I knew there was a deer trail on the bench just above us, but it wasn't worn as heavily as those below. And there was no way to position ourselves to watch both areas from above because we would be too far away from the saddle crossing. So, here we were, eyes focused on the area below. Still, every so often I cast a glance toward the bench above us, because you just never know about those bucks.

It's a lucky thing I did, because about an hour into the hunt, as I turned my head to look above, I caught a glimpse of a single deer slowly feeding around the side of the hill. It was about 30 yards away now and getting further from us. It had walked right past us, no more than 15 yards away, and we hadn't even heard it! The leaves were soaked from the previous day's rain and it was easy to walk without making much noise.

I thought it was a buck from the way it acted. It was alone, moving slowly and quietly, and constantly raising its head to look, smell, and listen. And besides that, I thought I had caught a glimpse of antlers when I first turned around -- possibly a forkhorn or a large spike. But I couldn't tell for sure.

I whispered to Jeff, who was about 15 feet away, and as he stood up to look, the deer jumped, snorted, and turned to look straight at us. We didn't move, and after about a 3-minute staring contest the deer turned to walk at a 45° angle back above us, nervously looking toward us every few seconds. I could now see the antlers; it was a spike buck. With Ohio's law requiring spikes to have 5 inch antlers, I was afraid to shoot. And the deer was moving further away. That's where Jeff saved the day! Moving quietly for a better view, he finally got a clear line of sight.

"Dad, those antlers are a good 5 inches, if not more," Jeff said excitedly.

"Are you sure," I asked?

"No doubt about it," he quickly and confidently responded!

The buck took a couple more steps to where I now had a good clear shot and I could now see the large spikes better myself. I squeezed the trigger on my trusty 16 gauge and the deer fell, not running at all. It had been a good, clean shot.

The day was a huge success! Jeff had gone on his first deer hunt. He had helped me get the deer. The rain had held off long enough to enjoy things. We would now have venison in the freezer all winter long. And best of all, Jeff and I were able to share a father-son experience that we'll long remember. He's sharp in the woods - maybe next year he'll get a big 10-pointer all by himself.

Oh yes, the antlers? They were big ones for a spike -- the left one 7 inches long and the right one 8 inches.

December 6, 1982 –

Though you couldn't tell it from the last two weeks' temperatures, Winter is nearly upon us. Soon after, the New Year comes in and we all make plans for 1983.

Our Wayne National Forest activities occur year round, though some jobs fall primarily in the Summer and others during Winter. We prepare a set of plans each October 1st (which is our fiscal year beginning date), outlining what we hope to accomplish in the following 12 months. Most of our tasks are determined by the way Congress and the President set up and approve the federal budget. We can't always just do what we think should be done. If they set aside a certain amount of money for timber projects, then the money must be used for timber projects. Our budget doesn't come in a lump sum, but is broken down, so much for timber, so much for recreation, some for wildlife management, some for fire fighting, and so on down the line.

Our budgets have been leaner the last couple of years and are expected to continue that way for the foreseeable future. Still, we've got a lot of work to do this year. Here are some of our major projects for 1983:

1) Reclamation - Work will continue toward reclaiming old, abandoned strip mines, mostly in the Athens area.

2) Recreation - We operate, maintain, and keep clean several recreation sites, including a campground at Burr Oak Cove, the Picnic Area and Boat Launch at Leith Run, the Lamping Homestead Recreation area in Monroe County, and other sites such as canoe access areas, hiking trails, horseback trails, etc.

3) Wildlife Management - Wildlife habitat improvement projects will be done. These include establishing small openings in the forest, maintaining old openings, creating new water ponds and maintaining old ones, and making plans for a small, 8 acre wetland along the Little Muskingum River in Washington County. This wetland will benefit waterfowl, aquatic life, and many other species of wildlife.

4) Forest Inventory - One of our Foresters will spend a large portion of his time collecting data about tree species, age, condition, volumes, etc. Approximately 10% of the Forest is inventoried each year. From this we determine which areas should be cut, planted, thinned, or improved in any way.

5) <u>Reforestation</u> - Over 200 acres will be planted to such tree species as white pine, tulip poplar, red oak, and others. Also, over 100 acres will be "cleared off" to allow sunlight to come in where young seedlings are already growing naturally.

6) <u>Timber Sales</u> - We will lay out, mark, and sell around 4 million board feet of timber this year; the locations are on both the Athens and the Marietta Units of our District.

7) <u>Firewood</u> - We still try to give out firewood permits for free home use, if possible. The demand has really been great, though, and it is difficult for us to keep up. Look for a change in the near future to where it will cost you to get a firewood permit.

8) <u>Minerals</u> - In the last three years, this has been our heaviest workload. We process well site locations, inspect them twice a year, and also monitor pipelines and road rights-of-way. Just in this Marietta Unit alone we have over 350 wells, 100 pipelines, and 30 road rights-of-way on National Forest land. Most of last year was spent getting compliance with well-site reclam-ation, and we were well pleased with the results. Now we're going to tackle another problem -- trying to get better quality roads to these well sites and to keep them maintained to a better standard.

These are our main jobs for the coming year. We've begun work on some of them already; the others will follow. We have many other assignments to work on also, including water quality sampling, fire fighting, surveying, checking certain areas for cultural artifacts (as required by law), genetic studies in tree planting areas, and many other related jobs.

Though our budget has been cut back, we've still got a lot to do -- only fewer people to help out. We're expecting a very busy 1983. If you have any questions about our upcoming projects, please stop by the office. We'd be glad to talk with you.

December 13, 1982 –

Again this year, the Nation has a Christmas tree at the Capitol that was cut from one of our National Forests. This year's tree, a 35-year old, 50-foot balsam fir, came from the Green Mountain National Forest in Vermont, near the small town of Rochester. And who should be present at the cutting ceremony but our own Geologist, Lynn Kantner.

Lynn periodically provides geologic advice and expertise to National Forests in Vermont, New Hampshire, Missouri, Illinois, and Indiana in addition to her work for the Wayne National Forest. She was able to watch the cutting ceremony, along with the other Green Mountain National Forest personnel. These ceremonies are quite impressive -- and well they should be, providing the Capitol with its traditional tree.

The governor of Vermont helped cut the tree, and there were short messages by Vermont's Fish and Game Commissioner, and the Green Mountain Forest Supervisor. The entire town of Rochester turned out for the send-off ceremony, and local citizens, schools, and organizations provided hundreds of hand-made decorations to go with the tree. Wouldn't it be nice if the Wayne National Forest could one day provide the Capitol Christmas tree?

The Forest Service is the agency responsible for coordinating the Christmas Tree Program. The tree is selected, several years in advance, by Forest Service officials and the Capitol Architect from Washington. The tree is selected from forests east of the Mississippi River, mainly because transporting one from the western U.S. would be very difficult. About 3 weeks before Christmas, the tree is carefully cut, removed from the woods, and transported in one piece to Washington, D.C. The labor, equipment, and transportation is donated by various groups and individuals.

Speaker of the House, Tip O'Neill, and his grandchildren will conduct this year's special lighting ceremony on December 15. There will be nearly 10,000 lights and ornaments on this year's tree.

Over the last 10 years, here are the trees that have served as our Capitol Christmas Tree:

1973 - White spruce - Allegheny National Forest - Pennsylvania

1974 – Fraser fir - Pisgah National Forest - North Carolina

1975 - Balsam fir - Ottawa National Forest - Michigan

1976 - Red spruce - Monongahela National Forest - West Virginia

1977 - White spruce - Nemadji State Forest - Minnesota

1978 - Norway spruce-Savage River State Forest-Maryland

1979 - White spruce - Nicolet National Forest - Wisconsin

1980 - White spruce - Green Mountain National Forest - Vermont

1981 - White spruce - Hiawatha National Forest - Michigan

1982 - Balsam fir - Green Mountain National Forest - Vermont

December 20, 1982 –

A couple of weeks ago I wrote about local projects that would be occurring during 1983 on the Wayne National Forest. We had a few inquiries about some of the work. Now our Forest Supervisor's Office has printed a newspaper tabloid (8 pages long) that details work plans for 1983 on the entire Forest. The tabloid, which was sent to people who have remained on our mailing list in recent years, serves as a public notice of activities which will occur this coming year. We have a few copies left here at the office, so if you'd like one, just let us know.

Below are a few of the Forest-wide activities which will happen in 1983.This includes the Ironton Ranger District (Gallia, Jackson, Lawrence, and Scioto Counties), as well as the Athens Ranger District:

Timber Harvest -- 9 million board feet of timber is scheduled to be cut out of a Forest total of 718 million board feet. Acreage wise, just 854 acres out of 175,000 will be affected. The areas to be cut are either mature, low quality, or with insect and disease problems. New, young, healthy trees will be regenerated once the timbering is completed. The average size of each individual cut area will be 22 acres.

Land Management Planning -- Last year public meetings were held and input was gathered to determine how people thought the Wayne National Forest should be managed. A very complex and detailed planning process is now going on, using this input gathered from the public as well as other information, which will help set direction for managing the Forest for the next 10 years.

Wetland Marshes -- Several small marshes are being designed, which will result in improved habitat for aquatic vegetation and animals. The water depth will be only 1-2 feet and will produce vegetation such as cattails and bulrushes. This, in turn, provides food and cover for ducks, herons, muskrats, sandpipers, turtles, frogs, and any number of other marsh dwellers. This is part of our overall wildlife management program, which includes non-game as well as game animals.

Fire Management -- As usual, wildfires will be put out as quickly as possible. The new twist is that we will set some of our own fires (controlled burns) to help us accomplish specific tasks. Like what? Well, for instance, to create or maintain "wildlife openings," which are so vital for wildlife habitat diversity, and to help establish oak seedlings by burning away competing vegetation.

Many other projects are planned for 1983. If you'd like more information on these or any other projects, please don't hesitate to call, write, or stop by the office on Newport Pike in Reno.

Our mailing address is:

Wayne National Forest, Route #1, Marietta, Ohio 45750; Phone # - 373-9055.

All of us at the Wayne National Forest wish you and yours a Merry Christmas and a very Happy New Year.

December 27, 1982 –

This week's column is written by Lynn Kantner, Geologist - U.S. Forest Service. Lynn is stationed here at the Marietta Office of the Wayne National Forest.

How Forest Service Lands Are Leased

You know, it seems like everything is changing -- rapidly. And everything seems to be getting more difficult and more complex. One theory is that we are moving (and have been for many years) from a simple, orderly state, to a progressively more complex, and therefore more disorderly and confusing situation.

If you've applied for a federal mineral lease lately, you would probably agree. There are a lot of stories to be told -- the original Mining Law of 1872, claim staking (and jumping), land patents, the "Government Oil and

Gas Lottery", etc. For now, let's just look at how oil and gas leasing is accomplished on federal land. ("Offshore Leasing" is still another story.)

The first point to remember is that all minerals beneath federal lands, whether those lands are National Forests, Parks, Wildlife Refuges, or whatever, are managed by the Bureau of Land Management (BLM). Thus locally, we have the situation where the surface is managed by the U.S. Forest Service and the subsurface by BLM. Now, that only applies when the minerals are also owned by the government, which in this area is only about 10% of the time. In the other 90%, private individuals have retained the mineral rights beneath the National Forest.

Federal oil and gas leases fall under three types: competitive, simultaneous (the "lottery system"), and over-the-counter noncompetitive applications. Here's the breakdown:

Competitive leases apply where government lands are located within a known geologic structure (kgs). For example, if the government had a tract of unleased land in the middle of "Yellow Knife Oil Field", it is a safe guess the lease would be bid competitively. Interested individuals or companies can ask that a tract of land or an entire area be opened for leasing. Leases are awarded to the bidder offering the highest per-acre cash bonus. Competitive leases have a 5-year primary term. Annual rent is $2 per acre and royalty is "sliding scale" based on production volume. This sliding scale royalty ranges from $12^1/_2$ percent to 25 percent. If drilling is successful and commercial quantities of oil and gas are found, the lease will be extended for as long as commercial production continues.

Land with expired or cancelled leases can be leased again only through <u>simultaneous</u> leasing procedures. Bi-monthly, beginning in January, BLM publishes a list of offered tracts. Applications for leases on these tracts that are received within 15 working days after the list is published are considered as "simultaneously" filed. New leases are issued based on a random selection (lottery) from the simultaneous applications. These leases have a 10-year primary term and require a $75 filing fee. The annual rent is $1 per acre for the first 5 years and $3 per acre thereafter. Royalty rate is $12^1/_2$ percent. The lease is extended for as long as commercial production continues.

Lands re-offered under the simultaneous leasing procedures that no one wants are lumped with lands never before having oil and gas applications. These tracts may be applied for <u>"over-the-counter"</u> (noncompetitively), that is, at the BLM office. Leases are awarded on a first-come, first-served basis for a 10-year primary term. The applicant must pay a $75 filing fee. Annual rent is $1 per acre for the first

5 years and \$3 per acre after that. Royalty is $12^1/_2$ percent.

It may sound complicated, and it is, but then nothing worthwhile is ever easy. Here is where you start. Write to:

U.S. Dept. of Interior - Bureau of Land Management, Eastern States Office, 350 South Pickett Street, Alexandria, VA 22304

You may also want to look at our land status maps here in the office, as several companies have already done.

www.ingramcontent.com/pod-product-compliance
Lightning Source LLC
Chambersburg PA
CBHW062137280526
45788CB00001B/196